Flight Training Workbook
for Private Pilots

by Dan K. Dyer

**The study guide and exercise workbook for the
FAA's Airplane Flying Handbook**

Flight Training Workbook for Private Pilots

655 Skyway Road, Suite 215
San Carlos, CA 94070

www.DyerFlight.com

ISBN: 978-0-578-05396-7

This book is a study guide and intended to allow flight students to better study and learn the material provided by the Federal Aviation Administration (FAA). The FAA has had no part in the creation of this workbook and should not be perceived to endorse the material contained herein. Similarly, the authors of this workbook do not intend for the workbook to replace or supplant any official pilot training material available from the FAA. Readers of this workbook should consult with their certificated flight instructor for help in determining what FAA materials are appropriate for study.

Note: This workbook refers to pages, diagrams, and chapters in the May 2004 version of the FAA's Airplane Flying Handbook. Prior versions of the FAA source text have different chapters and page numbering, as well as revised content matter. Please ensure that you use the May 2004 version while using this workbook.

October 2013 Edition

Acknowledgements

As a flight instructor, I developed a series of homework and reading assignments to use with my flight training students and with my ground school class. Those assignments ended up as a series of modules that covered both ground school knowledge and maneuvers preparation for flight training. The ground school modules have been published under the title "Ground School Workbook for Private Pilots". This workbook contains the remaining modules used to prepare and brief students for flight training.

I am grateful to the feedback and insights from a number of my flight and ground school students who used the materials contained herein as part of their training. Without their attention to detail and honest feedback, this workbook would have been substantially less effective. I have also enjoyed the encouragement and cooperation of many of the certified flight instructors with whom I work in San Carlos. I have been very fortunate to work in an environment in which there is a tremendous enthusiasm both for flying and for the flight training process, and it has been a privilege for me to be a part of that.

As someone passionate about flight training, I love to hear back from students and other instructors, especially when they find typos, errors, or other mistakes. Feel free to participate in the refinement of this training tool by sending any errors or corrections to me at Dan@DyerFlight.com.

Dan Dyer
Dyer Flight Training Tools

Table of Contents

Introduction   i

FTW-1 Introduction to Flight Training   1

FTW-2A Preflight Inspection   7

FTW-2B Ground Operations   11

FTW-3 Basic Flight Maneuvers   17

FTW-4A Slow Flight   23

FTW-4B Power-Off Stalls   27

FTW-4C Power-On Stalls   33

FTW-4D Spin Awareness   37

FTW-5A Takeoffs and Departure Climbs   43

FTW-5B Crosswind Takeoffs   49

FTW-5C Short-Field Takeoff   53

FTW-5D Soft-Field Takeoff   57

FTW-6 Ground Reference Maneuvers   61

FTW-7A Airport Traffic Patterns   71

FTW-7B Airport Procedures   75

FTW-8A Approaches and Landings   83

Table of Contents

FTW-8B Crosswind Approach and Landing   93

FTW-8C Short-Field Approach and Landing   97

FTW-8D Soft-Field Approach and Landing   101

FTW-8E Power-Off Accuracy Approaches   105

FTW-8F Emergency Approaches and Landings   109

FTW-8G Faulty Approaches and Landings   115

FTW-9 Steep Turns   119

FTW-10 Night Operations   123

FTW-11 Transition to Complex Airplanes   129

FTW-13 Transition to Tailwheel Airplanes   135

FTW-16A Emergency Landings   139

FTW-16B In-Flight Fires and Systems Malfunctions   145

FTW-16C Inadvertent VFR Flight into IMC   151

FTW-17 Recovery from Unusual Attitude   155

FTW-18 The Pilots Operating Handbook (POH)   161

Introduction

What is the Flight Training Workbook for Private Pilots?

Welcome to the Flight Training Workbook for Private Pilots, a study companion to the FAA's Airplane Flying Handbook. This workbook was written to help student pilots make better use of the FAA text and to better learn the material.

The FAA's Airplane Flying Handbook (referred to throughout this workbook as AFH) is a great book. It has good information on a wide variety of topics that pilots need to know about. It is revised regularly and constantly being improved. However, it can still read very much like a textbook. Some sections are dry. Some sections touch too lightly on important but complicated subject areas. Despite that, the AFH is still the best source for material on flight skills and maneuvers you will be tested on during your FAA Practical Test.

This book is a workbook. It is a set of exercises to be used in conjunction with the FAA source materials for training private pilots. Student pilots and flight instructors working together can use the sections in this workbook to build a better understanding of the topics required of a private pilot.

What FAA materials will I need to complete the exercises in this workbook?

You will need to have the FAA's main flight training textbook, the Airplane Flying Handbook (FAA-H-8083-3A). The latest version was released in 2004. The book covers all of the flight skills and maneuvers required of private pilots. Most of the exercises included in this workbook are built on information that you will find in the correct chapter and page of the AFH.

Occasionally, you will also need to refer to the FAA's Private Pilot Practical Test Standards (PTS) booklet for Airplane (FAA-S-8081-14AS). The PTS contains the performance standards that you will be tested on as a pilot. As you learn to fly, you'll be learning to fly to the performance standards contained in this document. Also, Section 7B refers to sections within the FAA's Aeronautical Information Manual (AIM), an excellent source for detailed procedural information that may not yet have made it into the Airplane Flying Handbook. The PTS and AIM can both be viewed online for free at http://www.faa.gov

Additionally, I've included four workbook sections from other key training references. The module on basic attitude/instrument flying includes study questions and exercises tied to Chapter 5 of the FAA's Instrument Flying Handbook (FAA-H-8083-15A). For those exercises, you'll need to either obtain a copy of the Instrument Flying Handbook (IFH) or view it online on the FAA's very usable website, http://www.faa.gov.

Finally, three workbook sections are tied to the airplane's Pilots Operating Handbook (POH). Learning the material in the POH for your airplane is an important part of flight training. Since all airplanes are different, you'll need to work with your flight instructor to understand how the questions in the POH workbook sections herein apply to your airplane.

Why was this workbook created?

As a student pilot, I was easily overwhelmed with the amount of material I was trying to learn. I often felt that there were too many sources of information and I didn't know which was the best source to use for each topic. On top of that, FAA source materials were often dry or poorly-worded, and it was easy to get lost in the details. Just reading the FAA materials didn't provide enough chances to actually use the new information in context or to connect it with prior lessons.

As an instructor I vowed to make the flight training process better for my students. I decided to create a set of exercises to walk a new student through everything that was needed of a private pilot.

What makes this workbook different from other quizzes or test prep guides?

This is a workbook. It is NOT a quiz booklet.

There are a number of quiz books or oral test prep guides available to student pilots. This book is different. The goal of this workbook is to teach. While you won't find any new reference material in this workbook, you will find yourself learning the material better through the use of guiding questions, practice questions, and discussion questions.

The goal of every exercise in this workbook is to increase your understanding of the material. Some of the questions are designed to lead you to the correct answer. Some are designed to make you think. Some questions are included specifically to draw your attention to minor points in the FAA text that could otherwise get overlooked. Working through these questions should leave you better informed than when you started. Some of the questions may include humorous answers – anything that helps you learn the material and enjoy the process.

This is in stark contrast from other training materials with quiz questions, or summary evaluation exercises. In those materials, you'll find questions that try to trick you or test multiple points at the same time. Their goal is not to teach but to evaluate. There is nothing wrong with materials of this type, but quizzes and tests should be used at the end of training, once learning has successfully happened. This workbook is to be used while you are still learning.

What kind of questions and exercises will I find in here?

Most of questions and exercises in the Flight Training Workbook for Private Pilots are self-explanatory and refer to information found directly in the AFH, IFH, and POH. There are multiple choice, short answer, fill-in-the-blanks, checkboxes, and circle answers. In some questions you'll draw your answer. I try to pick the style of question that best lends itself to making a connection in your mind, so you learn and remember the material.

In some cases I had to go beyond the scope of the FAA source text. Sometimes a guiding question can help set the tone for the information that follows. Other times, the FAA material does not go far enough in connecting some important ideas, and so I included probing questions to push you to think deeper.

Questions that don't directly tie to FAA source material are shaded and marked with special indicators.

Guess Questions

These questions prime your mental pump, so to speak. Their purpose is to get you thinking about the material that will come. A Guess Question may be on a topic that you have not yet been exposed to yet, but don't worry. The answers will guide you toward a way to think about the exercises that follow. Guess Questions are flagged with a question mark, as in the following example:

? 1. Most people are in a hurry to get to their destination, so why should student pilots practice flying as slowly as possible?

   a) To learn how to prolong the flight if they are going somewhere they don't want to go.
   b) To become proficient at flying the airplane at the slow end of its controllability range.
   c) To develop ways to avoid air speeding tickets.

Star Questions

Star Questions encourage you to take basic ideas from the FAA source text and to dig into a deeper understanding. They might ask you to correlate ideas from one aviation topic with another, or to tie together aspects of other modules to give you a deeper insight into a topic. Often Star Questions will attempt to relate flight training procedures concepts with concepts learned from ground school or from another portion of flight training. Appropriately, Star Questions are marked with a star symbol as in the following example:

2. How does wind affect a 180° ground reference turn made using a constant bank angle?

    a) The wind will distort the shape of the turn, unless other corrections are made.
    b) The various opposing effects of the wind cancel out over the 180° and the turn will be unaffected.
    c) The wind will always slow the groundspeed and reduce the turning radius.

Practice Exercises

Some flight skills are acquired through trial and error. In a few of the workbook sections, it is not enough to just read about something once. Really learning the material takes working through a practice problem or two. Sections of practice exercises are marked with a pencil symbol, as in the following example:

3. If V_{S0} for your airplane is 50 knots, and the current wind is at 10 knots with gusts up to 14 knots, what would be the fastest approach airspeed a pilot would use in making a short-field approach and landing?

    a) 52 knots.
    b) 67 knots.
    c) 74 knots.

Regardless of the type of question, your experience from working through the various questions and exercises in this workbook will be a deeper understanding of the material.

At the end of each section, the answers are included so that you can check your own work. Most of the questions you should have no trouble with but occasionally a question may seem too obscure. Once you see the correct answer, it may cue you to take a second look at the AFH to find what was missed.

How is this Flight Training Workbook organized?

The sections in this workbook have been put in order to match the AFH, chapter by chapter. In this way, Sections 1 through 16 match up to AFH's Chapters 1 through 16. When the text material is lengthy or covers many topics, I have tried to break it into smaller pieces to make it more manageable.

For example, AFH Chapter 8 covers Approach and Landing, which is quite a substantial topic. Beginning pilots could be overwhelmed with the full scope of the material. Therefore, I have divided the material from Chapter 8 into seven sections: Sections 8A, 8B, 8C, etc. For some students Section 8G may not be something they attempt until they have had some time to fully absorb a number of the other sections first.

Work through the material at your own pace and follow your interests as you find them. If you get bogged down by the material in one section, skip ahead to another more interesting section and come back to the tougher section later. Learning to fly is a never-ending process. There is always something more to learn. If you are not enjoying the process why learn to fly anyway?!

How should you use this workbook if you are training with a Certified Flight Instructor?

If you have already begun your flight training, and are working with a Certified Flight Instructor, you are both in luck. This workbook is great way for you to prepare for each lesson with your instructor. You'll arrive for each lesson feeling better prepared. And your instructor will be grateful that you are starting each lesson with a beginning grasp of the material.

Before each lesson you should:

1) Ask your instructor what flight training topics he or she would like you to study.
2) Find the workbook module on the assigned topic.
3) Read the FAA source material listed at the beginning of each module.
4) Work your way through the workbook exercises.
5) Compare your answers with the answers in the back of the book.
6) Arrive at your flight training lesson ready to be quizzed on what you've learned.

The exercises in this workbook should give you a great foundation for your training session with your flight instructor. It gets the basic training out of the way before the session and allows you and your flight instructor to focus on the ideas with which you had the most difficulty.

Although your flight instructor's training syllabus may cover the topics in a slightly different order than the modules contained in this workbook you can both still use the workbook as a checklist to make sure all important topics have been covered.

Pre-Solo Training	
Ground School	**Flight Training**
☐ [GSW-1] Introduction to Flying	☐ [FTW-1] Introduction to Flight Training
☐ [GSW-2] Aircraft Structure	☐ [FTW-2A] Preflight Inspection
☐ [GSW-3] Airfoils and the Principles of Flight	☐ [FTW-2B] Ground Operations
☐ [GSW-4A] Introduction to Aerodynamics	☐ [FTW-3] Basic Flight Maneuvers
☐ [GSW-4B] Aerodynamics in Flight	☐ [FTW-4A] Slow Flight
☐ [GSW-5] Flight Controls	☐ [FTW-4B] Power-Off Stalls
☐ [GSW-6A] Aircraft Engines and Systems – Part 1	☐ [FTW-4C] Power-On Stalls
☐ [GSW-6B] Aircraft Engines and Systems – Part 2	☐ [FTW-4D] Spin Awareness
☐ [GSW-7A] Pitot-Static Flight Instruments	☐ [FTW-5A] Takeoffs and Departure Climbs
☐ [GSW-7B] Other Flight Instruments	☐ [FTW-5B] Crosswind Takeoffs
☐ [GSW-8] Flight Manuals and Other Documents	☐ [FTW-6] Ground Reference Maneuvers
☐ [GSW-13] Airport Operations	☐ [FTW-7A] Airport Traffic Patterns
☐ [GSW-18A] Regulations for Student Solo Flight	☐ [FTW-7B] Airport Procedures
	☐ [FTW-8A] Approaches and Landings
	☐ [FTW-8B] Crosswind Approach and Landing
	☐ [FTW-8E] Power-Off Accuracy Approaches
	☐ [FTW-8F] Emergency Approaches and Landings
	☐ [FTW-8G] Faulty Approaches and Landing
	☐ [FTW-9] Steep Turns
	☐ [FTW-18] The Pilots Operating Handbook

Cross-Country Training	
Ground School	**Flight Training**
☐ [GSW-9] Weight and Balance	☐ [FTW-5C] Short-Field Takeoff
☐ [GSW-10A] Aircraft Performance	☐ [FTW-5D] Soft-Field Takeoff
☐ [GSW-10B] Aircraft Performance Charts	☐ [FTW-8C] Short-Field Approach and Landing
☐ [GSW-11A] Weather Theory – Atmospheric Circulation	☐ [FTW-8D] Soft-Field Approach and Landing
☐ [GSW-11B] Weather Theory – Moisture	☐ [FTW-16A] Emergency Landings
☐ [GSW-12] Aviation Weather Services	☐ [FTW-16B] In-flight Fires and Systems Malfunctions
☐ [GSW-14] Airspace	☐ [FTW-16C] Inadvertent VFR Flight into IMC
☐ [GSW-15A] Navigation – Part 1	☐ [FTW-17] Recovery from Unusual Attitude
☐ [GSW-15B] Navigation – Part 2	
☐ [GSW-15C] Navigation Practice Problems	
☐ [GSW-15D] Using VORs	
☐ [GSW-15E] Using ADFs and Bearing Pointers	
☐ [GSW-18B] Regulations for Solo Cross-Country Flight	

Practical Test Preparation	
Ground School	**Flight Training**
☐ [GSW-4C] Load Factor and Loading Considerations	☐ [FTW-10] Night Operations
☐ [GSW-16] Aeromedical Factors	☐ [FTW-11] Transition to Complex Airplanes
☐ [GSW-17] Aeronautical Decision Making	☐ [FTW-13] Transition to Tailwheel Airplanes
☐ [GSW-18C] Regulations for Private Pilot	

Introduction to Flight Training

<u>READING ASSIGNMENT</u>
AFH Chapter 1 – *Introduction to Flight Training*

Study Questions

1. Airmanship can be defined as

   • A sound acquaintance with _____,

   • The ability to operate an aircraft _____ both on the ground and in the air, and

   • The exercise of _____ that results in optimal operational _____ and _____.

2. The development of airmanship skills requires effort and dedication on the part of

   a) the student pilot.
   b) the flight instructor.
   c) both the student pilot and the flight instructor.

3. The goal of flight training is

   a) to pass the required practical test and become licensed.
   b) to learn how to fly a particular make and model of airplane.
   c) to make safe and competent pilots.

4. Through what document does the FAA prescribe safety standards for civil aviation?

   a) Congressional Safe Air Act of 1967.
   b) Title 14 of the Code of Federal Regulations (known formerly as Federal Aviation Regulations or FARs).
   c) The U.S. Constitution.

5. Determine which part of 14 CFR pertains to each of the listed topics.

   _____ General flight rules, including visual flight rules (VFR) and instrument flight rules (IFR).

   _____ The eligibility and training requirements for pilot certification.

   _____ Medical standards and procedures for issuing airmen medical certificates.

6. What forms the interface between the FAA's standard setting organization and the general aviation community?

   a) The pilot examiner.
   b) Local city and county governments.
   c) FSDOs.

7. Designated Pilot Examiners (DPEs) are

   a) FAA inspectors authorized to initiate enforcement action, investigate accidents, and perform surveillance activities on behalf of the FAA.
   b) private citizens designated by the FAA to accept applications and conduct practical tests leading to issuance of specific licenses and/or ratings.
   c) pilots trained to operate safely and competently in the National Airspace System.

8. How often must flight instructor certificates be renewed?

   _____

9. Most flight schools in the United States operate under the provisions of

   a) 14 CFR part 61.
   b) 14 CFR part 141.
   c) 14 CFR part 142.

10. Select the answers below that make the statements true.

    The FAA's Practical Test Standards booklet is a _teaching / testing_ document. It _does / does not_ contain descriptions of tasks, or information on how to perform maneuvers and procedures. A _flight instructor / DPE_ is responsible for training the pilot applicant to acceptable standards in _some of the / all_ subject matter areas included in the practical test standards.

    The pilot applicant should _be familiar with / memorize_ this book and refer to the standards it contains during _training / cross-country flight_ .

? 11. In your own words, what do you think "see and avoid" means?

   _____
   _____
   _____
   _____

12. What is the most effective strategy for collision avoidance?

    a) Formal medical training on the limitations of the human eye.
    b) Flight under Instrument Flight Rules (IFR).
    c) Proper clearing procedures combined with proper visual scanning techniques.

13. What is it called when a construction vehicle working in one part of an airport crosses onto a runway and creates a collision hazard with landing aircraft?

   _____

14. The absence of an operating control tower at an airport creates the need for

   a) a logbook authorization for "Uncontrolled Flight Ops."
   b) flight with a safety pilot.
   c) increased pilot vigilance.

★ 15. Which of the following are times that a student pilot and flight instructor should be aware of the potential for runway incursion? (Check all that apply.)

   ☐ Starting the engine while the aircraft is in the parking area.
   ☐ Taxiing along taxiways adjacent to runways.
   ☐ When taxiing onto a runway for takeoff.
   ☐ When doing aerial maneuvers in the flight practice area.
   ☐ On final approach to land on a runway.

16. Is flight at a low airspeed necessary to produce a stall?

   a) Yes.
   b) No.
   c) Only when flaps and landing gear are extended.

17. What have been the foundation of pilot standardization and cockpit safety for years?

   _____

18. Why is it important for flight instructors and student pilots to ensure positive transfer of the flight controls during training?

   a) FAA regulations require it.
   b) To be in synch with commercial airline procedures.
   c) Because there should never be any doubt as to who is flying the airplane at any time.

Excerpts from Title 14 Code Federal Regulations

§1.1 General Definitions

Unless the context requires otherwise, *Pilot in command* means the person who:

> (1) Has final authority and responsibility for the operation and safety of the flight;
> (2) Has been designated as pilot in command before or during the flight; and
> (3) Holds the appropriate category, class, and type rating, if appropriate, for the conduct of the flight.

§91.3 Responsibility and Authority of the Pilot in Command

> (a) The pilot in command of an aircraft is directly responsible for, and is the final authority as to, the operation of that aircraft.
> (b) In an in-flight emergency requiring immediate action, the pilot in command may deviate from any rule of this part to the extent required to meet that emergency.
> (c) Each pilot in command who deviates from a rule under paragraph (b) of this section shall, upon the request of the Administrator, send a written report of that deviation to the Administrator.

19. The "pilot in command" of a flight has _____ authority and _____ for the operation and safety of the flight.

20. If more than one licensed pilot is aboard the aircraft, which one is considered pilot in command?

    a) The one that boarded the airplane first.
    b) Whichever pilot is stationed in the main, left-side pilot seat.
    c) The one designated as pilot in command before or during the flight.

21. A pilot can be considered pilot in command of a flight regardless of whether that pilot holds the appropriate ratings for the conduct of the flight.

    a) True.
    b) False.

22. Can the pilot in command be held directly responsible for the operation of the aircraft?

    a) No.
    b) Yes, but only when carrying passengers.
    c) Yes.

23. In the event of an in-flight emergency requiring immediate action, what can the pilot in command do?

    _____
    _____
    _____

24. Is the pilot in command authorized to violate federal aviation regulations?

    a) Yes, if the pilot believes it is required to ensure the safety of the flight in an emergency.

    b) Yes, if an air traffic controller agrees and issues a corresponding clearance.

    c) No. Pilots must obey all laws regardless of its impact on the safety of the flight.

25. Each pilot in command who deviates from a rule shall, _____ , send a written report of that deviation to the Administrator (FAA).

Answers to Study Questions

1. principles of flight
    with competence and precision
    sound judgment
    safety
    efficiency

2. c

3. c

4. b

5. Part 91
    Part 61
    Part 67

6. c

7. b

8. every 24 calendar months

9. a

10. testing
    does not
    flight instructor
    all
    be familiar with
    training

11. scanning for other air traffic, being vigilant, and ensuring that your flight path remains clear of other air traffic

12. c

13. runway incursion

14. c

15. ☐ Starting the engine while the aircraft is in the parking area.
    ☒ Taxiing along taxiways adjacent to runways.
    ☒ When taxiing onto a runway for takeoff.
    ☐ When doing aerial maneuvers in the flight practice area.
    ☒ On final approach to land on a runway.

16. b

17. checklists

18. c

19. final
    responsibility

20. c

21. b (false)

22. c

23. may deviate from any rule to the extent required to meet that emergency

24. a

25. upon the request of the Adminstrator

Preflight Inspection

READING ASSIGNMENT
AFH Pages 2-1 to 2-7 – "Visual Inspection" through "Cockpit Management"

Study Questions

1. What are the two purposes of the preflight inspection?

   _____

   _____

2. Airplane maintenance logbooks are required to be kept aboard the airplane when it is operated.

   a) True.
   b) False.

3. The preflight inspection should begin

   a) while approaching the airplane on the ramp.
   b) from inside the cockpit.
   c) with a look under the engine cowling.

4. Why would a sticky cockpit door or water on the cockpit floor be a cause for concern?

   a) The pilots of messy aircraft are subject to penalties from the FAA.
   b) The aircraft will not fly as efficiently.
   c) Misalignment of the door or fuselage can be a sign of structural damage.

5. Which of the following would indicate a problem with the magnetic compass? (Check all that apply.)

   ☐ Compass instrument face full of fluid
   ☐ Bubbles in the compass fluid
   ☐ A 50/50 balance of air and fluid inside the compass

6. During preflight inspection, what should be the proper indications on the airspeed indicator, vertical speed indicator, and altimeter?

   a) Airspeed = 75 kts, Vertical speed = 100 fpm, Altimeter = 0 feet.
   b) Airspeed = 0 kts, Vertical speed = 0 fpm, Altimeter = within 75 feet of field elevation.
   c) Airspeed = 0 kts, Vertical speed = 0 fpm, Altimeter = 0 feet.

7. The presence of black oxide streaks around rivets is

   a) normal, and should be on no concern.
   b) indicative of loose or sheared aluminum rivets.
   c) evidence of a probable fuel leak.

8. AVGAS evaporates _____, but jet fuel is _____ to evaporate and leaves behind an oily smudge.

9. What is the best way to minimize the opportunity for water to condense in the fuel tanks?

    a) Use rubber fuel tank seals and elastic fuel caps and vents.
    b) Only fuel the aircraft in the mornings before the first flight of the day.
    c) Fill the tanks completely after the last flight of the day.

10. Tires with bulges, exposed cord, or cracked sidewalls should be

    a) considered unairworthy.
    b) examined frequently for signs of additional wear and tear.
    c) rotated carefully, and taxi speeds reduced for safety.

11. Which of the following would be cause for concern with the brakes and brake systems? (Check all that apply.)

    ☐ Wheels that move freely if aircraft is pulled with brakes released
    ☐ Loose nuts or bolts
    ☐ Signs of hydraulic fluid leakage
    ☐ Wheel fairing removed
    ☐ Rust and corrosion
    ☐ Brake pad wear or cracks

12. What is the purpose of the propeller spinner (cone-shaped point attached to center of spinning propeller)?

    a) To channel air into the engine air intakes for better cooling.
    b) To balance the spinning propeller.
    c) To make the aircraft appear chic and more modern.

13. A cracked spinner is _____.

Answers to Study Questions

1. to determine that the aircraft is safe to fly
   to determine that the aircraft is legal to fly

2. b (false)

3. a

4. c

5. ☐ Compass instrument face full of fluid
   ☒ Bubbles in the compass fluid
   ☒ A 50/50 balance of air and fluid inside the compass

6. b

7. b

8. quickly
   slower

9. c

10. a

11. ☐ Wheels that move freely if aircraft is pulled with brakes released
    ☒ Loose nuts or bolts
    ☒ Signs of hydraulic fluid leakage
    ☐ Wheel fairing removed
    ☒ Rust and corrosion
    ☒ Brake pad wear or cracks

12. a

13. unairworthy

Ground Operations

FTW-2B

READING ASSIGNMENT
AFH Pages 2-7 to 2-12 – "Ground Operations" through "Securing and Servicing"

Study Questions

1. Why do you think ground operations might be more dangerous than flight operations?

   a) The proximity to the ground makes for a dangerous dynamic resonance with the propeller.
   b) Winds at the surface are usually stronger than at altitude.
   c) Spinning propellers are often hard to see and are at exactly the height to be a danger to people and property on the surface of the airport.

2. All engine start procedures are the same from one single-engine aircraft to the next.

   a) True.
   b) False.

3. On engine start and at run up, how should the airplane be positioned?

   a) Nose pointing toward magnetic north.
   b) Nose pointed directly away from open hangar doors or people that could be damaged by propeller blast (or "propwash").
   c) In such a manner that nothing is or will be near the vicinity of the moving propeller, and that nothing is affected by the propeller blast.

4. How loud should the pilot yell "Clear" before starting the airplane?

   a) Normal speaking volume, so as not to be embarrassed or call attention to oneself.
   b) Loud enough to be heard at a distance of 10 feet.
   c) As loud as possible. Let there be no confusion to anyone in the vicinity that the propeller is about to start moving and everyone should remain clear.

5. What standard procedure allows the pilot to make a prompt response if the engine falters or if engine RPM is excessive at engine start?

   a) The pilot should always one hand free and resting in his or her lap in case throttle changes are required.
   b) The pilot should always keep one hand on the throttle during engine start (as well as while taxiing, and during takeoff and landing).
   c) The pilot should use a grease pencil and mark the proper throttle setting for engine start on the throttle control rod.

6. Why is it highly undesirable to allow the engine to race immediately after start?

   a) There is insufficient lubrication until the oil pressure rises.
   b) High RPM settings can damage avionics or other electrical devices.
   c) In warm temperatures, the engine is exposed to mechanical distress until it cools to normal operating temperatures.

7. How should hand propping an airplane be accomplished?

   a) With great care, especially when attempted alone.
   b) Only when absolutely necessary, and then with a minimum of two people, both familiar with the airplane and hand propping techniques.
   c) Only on soft, loose surfaces that provide a soft impact in case the person in front of the propeller falls.

8. When taxiing an airplane, where should the pilots eyes be?

   _____

   _____

   _____

9. At what speed should an airplane be taxied?

   a) At a speed slow enough that the airspeed indicator needle doesn't move.
   b) At a speed slow enough to recognize potential hazards in time to avoid them.
   c) At any speed provided the pilot can maintain control through active, continuous application of the brakes

10. Unless necessary to move around obstructions or other airplanes, what should a pilot observe while taxiing?

    a) Yellow taxiway centerline stripes.
    b) At least one foot clearance from any person, hangar, vehicle, or tower.
    c) Steady acceleration into a turn, with steady braking coming out of a turn.

11. How do aileron movements affect taxiing direction?

    a) They do not.
    b) Ailerons are used to help turn the aircraft into the wind.
    c) Up aileron movements are associated with left turns; down aileron with right turns.

 12. Why is extra engine power required to start the airplane moving forward or in a turn?

    a) To overcome friction and inertia.
    b) To overcome left turning tendencies.
    c) To improve airflow over the elevator and increase control effectiveness.

13. When should the pilot perform a brake test?

    a) On the takeoff roll down the runway.
    b) After ensuring adequate engine performance in the run-up area.
    c) When first beginning to taxi.

14. In moderate to strong headwinds, the elevator control on a nose-wheel aircraft should be held _____, and on a tailwheel aircraft the control should be held in the _____ position to keep the tail down.

15. How can the pilot prevent against overheating the brakes, when taxiing downwind?
    a) Keep engine power to a minimum.
    b) Gently turn the aircraft from side to side to slow forward motion.
    c) Add coolant to the brake system.

16. What is the only surface maneuver that could require the contradictory combination of throttle power above idle and simultaneous application of brakes?
    a) Slowing to stop on an aborted takeoff.
    b) Sharps turns at low speed.
    c) Centerline control on taxiways with minimal lateral clearance.

17. When taxiing into a quartering headwind, what direction should the aileron on the upwind side be held and why?
    a) Up, to reduce the lifting action of the wing and reduce the effect of the wind striking the wing.
    b) Up, to increase ground clearance on the side of the plane closest to the wind.
    c) Down, to provide downward pressure to keep the wing from lifting up.

18. If taxiing into a right quartering headwind in an airplane with a nosewheel, the elevator should be neutral and the aileron on the upwind side should be up. Circle the flight control movements that accomplish elevator neutral – upwind aileron up.

Elevator Movement	Aileron Movement
Climb	Into the wind
Level	Away from the wind
Dive	

19. With wind coming from the back and left, the elevator should be down and the upwind aileron should be down. Circle the flight control movements that accomplish elevator down – upwind aileron down.

Elevator Movement	Aileron Movement
Climb	Into the wind
Level	Away from the wind
Dive	

20. Describe the factors that influence the positioning of the aircraft for a Before Takeoff Check (also known as a "runup").

   _____
   _____
   _____
   _____
   _____
   _____

21. How should the runup be performed?

   a) According to the specifications set down in the Federal Aviation Regulations.
   b) Using the before takeoff checklist provided by the airplane manufacturer or operator.
   c) In the same manner on every airplane as aircraft engines are nearly identical.

22. Why is the after-landing check only performed after the airplane is brought to a complete stop clear of the active runway?

   a) To give full attention to controlling the airplane during the landing roll.
   b) To avoid overstressing the flap actuator motor.
   c) Retraction of flaps or landing gear on the runway requires special control tower authorization.

23. In which order is the aircraft engine shutdown, mixture to idle/cutoff then ignition switch off, or ignition switch off then mixture to idle/cutoff?

   a) Either way is fine.
   b) Ignition switch off to kill the spark plugs, then fuel to idle/cutoff to cut fuel flow to the engine.
   c) Fuel to idle/cutoff to starve the engine of fuel, then after the engine has stopped ignition switch to off to prevent spark.

24. Why is it a good operating practice to fill the tanks to the top at the end of the day?

   _____
   _____
   _____

Answers to Study Questions

1. c
2. b (false)
3. c
4. c
5. b
6. a
7. b
8. outside the airplane, looking to the sides, as well as the front
9. b
10. a
11. a
12. a
13. c
14. neutral
    aft

15. a
16. b
17. a
18. Level   Into the wind
19. Dive   Away from the wind
20. Aircraft should be clear of other aircraft
    Nothing behind the aircraft that might be damaged by prop blast
    Headed as nearly into the wind as possible
    Nosewheel/tailwheel aligned fore and aft
21. b
22. a
23. c
24. Filling the tanks to the top at the end of the day prevents water condensation from forming overnight.

READING ASSIGNMENT

AFH Chapter 3 – *Basic Flight Maneuvers*

Study Questions

1. How should the flight controls be held by the pilot?

   a) Lightly, with the fingers, not grabbed or squeezed.
   b) Tightly, to prevent loss of control in flight.
   c) Lightly while enroute, and tightly within 500 feet of the ground.

2. Describe the proper foot position for a pilot while flying?

   _____
   _____
   _____
   _____

3. When the sound level of the air flowing past the cabin increases, it indicates that

   a) airspeed is increasing.
   b) airspeed is decreasing.
   c) the airplane is probably in a climb.

4. Attitude flying for VFR pilots means visually establishing the airplane's attitude with reference to

   a) the gyroscopic attitude instruments.
   b) the position and angle of the sun.
   c) the natural horizon.

5. In attitude flying, airplane control is composed of what four components?

   _____
   _____
   _____
   _____

6. Complete the primary rule of attitude flying.

Airplane Flight Attitude	+	Engine Power Setting	=	

7. How should a pilot establish and maintain proper pitch and bank attitude?

   a) By staring inside at the attitude indicator.
   b) By relaxing the controls until the trim flies the airplane.
   c) By using to the natural horizon, with a least 90% of the pilot's attention looking outside.

8. When the flight instruments indicate the need for a correction, a specific amount of correction must be determined (e.g., raise the nose up another 1°) and then applied with reference to

   _____

   _____

9. How should a pilot monitor the performance (altitude, airspeed, heading) of the airplane?

   a) With crosscheck between the flight instruments and ATC reports of airspeed, altitude, and heading.
   b) With continuous attention, and reactive control changes at the first indication of needle variation.
   c) With numerous quick glances at the flight instruments, but no more than 10% of the pilot's attention inside the cockpit.

10. Which affords the pilot a greater degree of accuracy with regard to maintaining a desired airplane attitude?

    a) The attitude indicator.
    b) The turn and slip indicator (or turn coordinator).
    c) The natural horizon.

11. The most common error made by the beginning student is to make pitch and bank corrections

    a) using electronic controls.
    b) while still looking inside the cockpit.
    c) too gradually.

12. Level flight is a matter of consciously fixing the relationship of the position of _____ of the

    airplane used as a reference point, with _____.

13. What is the VFR pilot's primary reference source for pitch information?

    a) The natural horizon.
    b) The attitude indicator.
    c) The altimeter.

14. Which of the following are common errors for pilots attempting straight-and-level flight?

    ☐ Habitually flying with one wing high.
    ☐ Attempting to correct airplane attitude using flight instruments instead of outside visual references.
    ☐ Too tight a grip on the flight controls resulting in overcontrolling or lack of feel.
    ☐ Too much time focused outside the aircraft and not enough reading the flight instruments..

15. To avoid the common error of overcontrolling the airplane with trim adjustments, the pilot must learn to

   a) use the trim to establish or correct airplane attitude.
   b) fly the airplane using the trim tabs.
   c) establish and hold the desired attitude using the primary flight controls, verify performance with the flight instruments, and only then apply trim to relieve control pressures.

16. Define the angle of bank ranges for the following turns:
   Shallow turns _____
   Medium turns _____
   Steep turns _____

17. Once the airplane wings are banked into a shallow turn, all pressure applied to the aileron may be relaxed, and the airplane will remain at the selected bank.

   a) True.
   b) False.

18. In a turn, all the lifting force provided by the wings gets split into what two components?

   a) Lift and adverse yaw.
   b) Gravity.
   c) Vertical lift component and horizontal lift component.

19. After a medium banked turn has been established, what aileron control inputs are required?

   a) Some opposite aileron will be required to maintain the bank angle.
   b) The aileron pressure may be relaxed and the control wheel returned to neutral.
   c) Full opposite aileron will be required to offset overbanking tendency.

20. In order to maintain altitude in a constant speed turn, the total amount of lift must be _____.

★ 21. In a steep turn, why does the outside wing develop more lift than the inside wing?

   _____
   _____
   _____

22. Which will result in the smallest radius of turn?

   a) 5° angle of bank.
   b) 15° angle of bank.
   c) 30° angle of bank.

23. Which will result in the smallest radius of turn?

   a) 70 knots.
   b) 85 knots.
   c) 110 knots.

24. Which way should the pilot lean in a turn?

    a) Away from the turn, to keep the body upright in relation to the ground.
    b) Into the turn, to improve forward visibility.
    c) The pilot should not lean in a turn, as this distorts his or her ability to properly interpret outside references.

25. In a 20° banked turn, how far in advance of the desired heading should the pilot begin to roll out and level the wings?

    a) 5°.
    b) 10°.
    c) 20°.

26. A common error in the performance of level medium-bank turns is continuing to hold _____ in the turn.

27. Why is the normal climb speed generally somewhat faster than the airplane's speed for best rate of climb?

    a) To gain altitude somewhat more quickly.
    b) The negative pressure of aileron inputs limit lift.
    c) For better engine cooling and forward visibility.

 28. How can a pilot use trim in a climb?

    a) The same way as in straight and level flight. Fly a chosen pitch attitude in reference to the horizon, then use trim to remove the control pressures.
    b) From straight and level flight, begin the climb by simultaneously adding power and moving the trim control toward a nose up attitude.
    c) Trim should only be used to maintain straight and level flight.

29. How will the altitude gained in a climbing turn compare to the altitude gained in a straight climb?

    a) A straight climb will always yield a greater altitude gain than a climbing turn.
    b) As the radius of the turn tightens, the aircraft in a climbing turn will gain altitude more quickly than in a straight climb.
    c) The rate of climb is controlled only by throttle setting and airspeed and angle of bank have no impact.

30. The target descent rate in a partial power descent should be _____.

 31. Which airplane will glide at a steeper descent angle, Airplane A with a glide ratio of 10 to 1, or Airplane B with a glide ratio of 8.5 to 1?

    a) Airplane A
    b) Airplane B
    c) It is not possible to determine from the given information.

Answers to Study Questions

1. a

2. feet resting comfortably on the floor with the ball of each foot touching the pedal

3. a

4. c

5. pitch control
   bank control
   power control
   trim

6. performance

7. c

8. the natural horizon

9. c

10. c

11. b

12. some portion
    the horizon

13. a

14. ☒ Habitually flying with one wing high.
    ☒ Attempting to correct airplane attitude using flight instruments instead of outside visual references.
    ☒ Too tight a grip on the flight controls resulting in overcontrolling or lack of feel.
    ☐ Too much time focused outside the aircraft and not enough reading the flight instruments..

15. c

16. less than 20°
    20° to 45°
    45° or more

17. b. False

18. c

19. b

20. increased

21. the outside wing travels faster (longer distance in the same time) and develops more lift

22. c

23. a

24. c

25. b

26. rudder

27. c

28. a

29. a

30. 400 to 500 feet per minute

31. b

Slow Flight

READING ASSIGNMENT
AFH Pages 4-1 to 4-2 – "Introduction" through
                         "Flight at Minimum Controllable Airspeed"
PTS VIII.A – Maneuvering during Slow Flight

Study Questions

AFH Pages 4-1 to 4-2 – "Introduction" through "Flight at Minimum Controllable Airspeed"

1. Most people are in a hurry to get to their destination, so why should student pilots practice flying as slowly as possible?

   a) To learn how to prolong the flight if they are going somewhere they don't want to go.
   b) To become proficient at flying the airplane at the slow end of its controllability range.
   c) To develop ways to avoid air speeding tickets.

2. Fill in the blanks to complete the two uses of the term "slow flight."

   • Maneuvering the airplane at lower airspeeds to determine characteristic control responses at speeds appropriate to takeoff, departure, _____, and go around.

   • Maneuvering the airplane at the _____ airspeed at which the airplane is capable of maintaining controlled flight without the indications of a _____.

3. As airspeed slows during slow flight, how does the effectiveness of the controls change?

   a) Control effectiveness decreases disproportionately as airspeed decreases.
   b) The flight controls become more sensitive and the airplane responds more quickly to pilot input.
   c) The control effectiveness gradually increases as disrupting airflow over the wing decreases.

4. Minimum controllable airspeed (MCA) is

   a) the airspeed at which the controls are moved only minimally to control the airplane.
   b) the airspeed specified on the airworthiness certificate for cruise flight at minimum gross weight.
   c) the speed at which any further increase in angle of attack or reduction in power will cause an immediate stall.

5. Which of the following are characteristics of flight at very low airspeeds? (Check all that apply.)

   ☐ Sloppy controls
   ☐ Stuttering or irregular engine power
   ☐ Ragged response to control movements
   ☐ Difficulty maintaining altitude
   ☐ Rigid aileron pressures

6. Read the following action items and put them in the correct order to use when demonstrating slow flight (i.e., flight at MCA). Put 1 next to the item which is to be done first, 2 next to the second item, etc.

_____ After the airspeed has slowed to below V_{FE}, extend flaps in stages until landing configuration is established.

_____ Gradually reduce throttle from the cruise power setting to allow the aircraft to begin slowing while gradually raising the nose to hold altitude.

_____ Note changes in flight characteristics (feel of the controls, sounds of the airflow)

_____ As the airspeed slows below V_x/V_y, increase power to overcome induced drag and hold altitude.

_____ Establish a safe altitude and perform clearing turns to ensure the area is clear of other aircraft.

7. Throughout the maneuver, the flight conditions are constantly changing. Fill in the blanks to indicate how the pilot should be adjusting the controls during "slow flight."

   • Application of the _____ to maintain coordinated flight throughout the various nose-high pitch attitudes and high power settings.

   • _____ the airplane as often as necessary to reduce control pressures and make precise control of the aircraft easier.

   • Pitch used to carefully control _____, to prevent decay from increased total drag when operating below minimum drag speed.

   • Adjust the _____ as necessary to maintain altitude (or to establish a climb or descent as desired.)

   • Ailerons used as needed to keep the wings _____.

8. Which of the following mantras can help the pilot remember the correct control adjustments required during slow flight?

   a) "Altitude, pitch, airspeed."
   b) "Pitch for airspeed, power for altitude, wings level, coordinated."
   c) "Trim for altitude, power for airspeed, rudder for level, ailerons for heading."

9. After straight and level slow flight has been established, turns can be accomplished, but power and pitch attitude may need to be increased to

   a) allow for abrupt control movements.
   b) maintain the airspeed and altitude.
   c) enter a stall.

10. Which of the following are common errors of pilots performing slow flight? (Check all that apply.)

   ☐ Fixation on the airspeed indicator (or any flight instrument)
   ☐ Division of attention between airplane control and orientation (attitude/heading)
   ☐ Failure to anticipate changes in lift as flaps are extended or retracted
   ☐ Lack of coordination in turns (due failure to compensate for adverse yaw)
   ☐ Failure to perform clearing turns
   ☐ Over-reliance on power (throttle) changes for maintaining altitude

PTS VIII.A – Maneuvering during Slow Flight

11. What airspeed does the PTS specify for the demonstration of slow flight?

    a) $V_Y \pm 10$ knots.
    b) An airspeed at which any further increase in angle of attack or reduction in power would result in an immediate stall.
    c) 95 knots.

12. What airplane configuration should be used to demonstrate slow flight?

    a) Flaps fully extended.
    b) Flaps and landing gear fully retracted.
    c) The configuration specified by the examiner.

13. Where should the pilot's attention be during slow flight?

    a) The airspeed indicator
    b) The airspeed indicator, altimeter, heading indicator, and inclinometer.
    c) Divided between airplane control (inside) and orientation (outside).

 14. Following the performance of slow flight, how should the pilot end the maneuver?

    a) Nose down to trade altitude for airspeed, returning to normal cruise speed in the descent.
    b) Return power to cruise setting, using pitch to maintain altitude as the airspeed increases and the flaps are retracted.
    c) Simulate engine failure by pulling the mixture control knob to idle/cutoff.

Answers to Study Questions

1. b

2. landing approach
   slowest
   stall

3. a

4. c

5. ☒ Sloppy controls
   ☐ Stuttering or irregular engine power
   ☒ Ragged response to control movements
   ☒ Difficulty maintaining altitude
   ☐ Rigid aileron pressures

6. 3
   2
   5
   4
   1

7. rudder
   Retrim
   airspeed
   power
   level

8. b

9. b

10. ☒ Fixation on the airspeed indicator (or any flight instrument)
    ☐ Division of attention between airplane control and orientation (attitude/heading)
    ☒ Failure to anticipate changes in lift as flaps are extended or retracted
    ☒ Lack of coordination in turns (due failure to compensate for adverse yaw)
    ☒ Failure to perform clearing turns
    ☐ Over-reliance on power (throttle) changes for maintaining altitude

11. b

12. c

13. c

14. b

Power-Off Stalls

READING ASSIGNMENT
AFH Pages 4-3 to 4-8 – "Stalls" through "Full Stalls Power-Off"
PTS VIII.B – Power-Off Stalls

Study Questions

AFH Pages 4-3 to 4-8 – "Stalls" through "Full Stalls Power-Off"

? 1. What are the two reasons that student pilots practice making the airplane wings stall during private pilot training? (Check two answers only).

    ☐ To develop quick reflex responses to recover from a stall should one ever occur in flight
    ☐ To add a touch of excitement to flight training, which can be often dull and uneventful
    ☐ To meet FAA performance standards requiring pilots to be able to rapidly lose altitude in the event of an emergency
    ☐ To learn to recognize an impending stall before it happens, so that prompt action can be taken to prevent a stall from occurring

2. When does a stall occur?

    a) When the engine is starved of fuel, either intentionally or unintentionally.
    b) When the smooth airflow over the airplane's wing is disrupted and lift degenerates rapidly.
    c) Only when airspeeds drop below the bottom of the green arc on the airspeed indicator.

3. What are the various warnings of an approaching stall condition?

    a) Sudden engine silence, control mushiness, and violent shaking.
    b) Control mushiness, buffeting, and warning horn sounding.
    c) Buffeting, and steadily increasing sounds of air flow over the fuselage.

4. What are the three steps of a stall recovery?

    1. _____
    2. _____
    3. _____

5. While not the key aspect of a safe stall recovery, smooth application of power will

    a) aid in increasing the airplane's airspeed to minimize altitude loss.
    b) tend to yaw the aircraft to the right and may induce a spin.
    c) end the stall, regardless of whether the airplane angle of attack is changed.

6. Practicing power-off stalls can show the student pilot what can happen

   a) during takeoff and climb.
   b) during approach and landing.
   c) during descent from cruise altitude.

7. Stall accidents usually result from

   a) excessive power application during stall recovery.
   b) too much repeated stall practice.
   c) an inadvertent stall too low to the ground.

 8. The point of practicing stalls is to learn

   a) how to make the airplane exceed its load limitations.
   b) how to set up the aircraft for a possible spin.
   c) how to detect a stall before it happens, and how to recover from one if necessary.

9. The airplane shown below has been designed with wing washout, where the angle of attack at the wingtips has been designed to be less than the angle of attack at the root of the wings. Shade the part of the wings that would first experience the disruptive airflows in a stall.

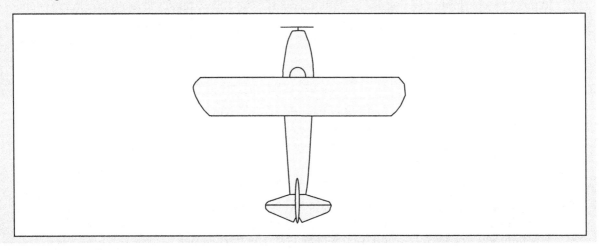

10. Wing washout is a design feature that results in

    a) the tips of the wings stalling before the root.
    b) the root of the wings stalling before the wing tips.
    c) the airplane nose to drop cleanly ("washing out") out of the stall.

11. Because of wing washout, the ailerons still have some control and can

    a) be used carefully to level the wings, provided excessive control inputs are not used.
    b) support the airplane in level flight even if the wing roots have stalled.
    c) be used instead of the rudder to maintain coordinated flight.

12. Rudder coordination is critical both in the entry and recovery from a stall in order to prevent

    a) excessive pitch changes.
    b) the development of yawing moments which could result in a spin.
    c) rudder stall.

13. A stall can occur

    a) at any airspeed, in any attitude, or at any power setting.
    b) only at nose-high attitudes.
    c) only at airspeeds slower than V_X or V_Y.

14. In practicing some stalls, the plane may appear to be cross-controlled, even though that is the appropriate way to maintain a constant pitch and bank attitude.

    a) True.
    b) False.

15. Define the following terms:

    cross-controlled _____

    imminent stall_____

16. In practicing approaches to stalls, recovery is initiated

    a) as soon as the first buffeting or partial control loss is noted.
    b) after full stall has occurred.
    c) when the pilot has positive indication of a nose drop.

17. During a power-off stall, directional control should be maintained with the _____ and the wings held level by use of the _____.

18. Which of the following could be stall indications when practicing power-off stalls? (Check all that apply.)

    ☐ Full up elevator
    ☐ High descent rate
    ☐ Uncontrollable nose-down pitching
    ☐ Possible buffeting

19. Recovering from a power-off stall should be accomplished by reducing the angle of attack, smoothly applying maximum available _____ and using coordinated application of the _____ to overcome engine torque.

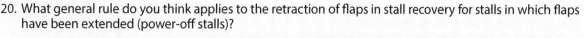

20. What general rule do you think applies to the retraction of flaps in stall recovery for stalls in which flaps have been extended (power-off stalls)?

    a) Retract the flaps at the first indication of an approaching stall.
    b) Bring the flaps up whenever the pitch attitude has recovered to within 5° of level cruise attitude.
    c) Don't retract the last 10° or 20° of flaps until 1) the airplane is climbing (positive indication of climb) and 2) airspeed is sufficient to maintain the climb (at or above V_R).

21. How should a practice stall recovery terminate?

    a) In a constant rate descent to the original altitude.
    b) In straight and level cruise flight.
    c) In a climb (often until reaching the original altitude).

PTS VIII.B – Power-Off Stalls

22. If demonstrating a stall in straight flight, the PTS says the pilot must maintain their heading within _____°
while inducing the stall. If demonstrating a turning stall, the angle of bank must be maintained within

    _____°.

23. The pilot examiner will expect the aircraft to attain what airspeed before the pilot retracts the final amount of flaps?

    a) V_X or V_Y.
    b) Cruise climb airspeed.
    c) MCA.

Answers to Study Questions

1. ☒ To develop quick reflex responses to recover from a stall should one ever occur in flight

   ☐ To add a touch of excitement to flight training, which can be often dull and uneventful

   ☐ To meet FAA performance standards requiring pilots to be able to rapidly lose altitude in the event of an emergency

   ☒ To learn to recognize an impending stall before it happens, so that prompt action can be taken to prevent a stall from occurring

2. b

3. b

4. 1) Pitch down to reduce angle of attack,
   2) increase power to maximum allowable, and
   3) carefully regain straight and level flight.

5. a

6. b

7. c

8. c

9.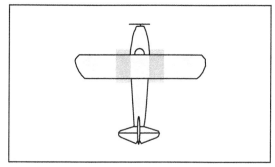

10. b

11. a

12. b

13. a

14. a (true)

15. aileron pressure in one direction, rudder pressure in the opposite direction
    the airplane is approaching a stall, but not allowed to completely stall

16. a

17. rudder
    ailerons

18. ☒ Full up elevator
    ☒ High descent
    ☒ Uncontrollable nose-down pitching
    ☒ Possible buffeting

19. power
    rudder

20. c

21. c

22. 10°
    10°

23. a

Power-On Stalls

READING ASSIGNMENT

AFH Pages 4-8 to 4-12 – "Full Stalls Power-On" through "Elevator Trim Stall"
PTS VIII.C – Power-On Stalls

Study Questions

AFH Pages 4-8 to 4-12 – "Full Stalls Power-On" through "Elevator Trim Stall"

1. After establishing the takeoff or climb configuration, demonstration of a power-on stall (i.e., takeoff stall or departure stall) begins by

   a) slowing the airplane to normal lift-off speed (e.g., V_R).
   b) bringing the nose smoothly upward to an attitude obviously impossible for the airplane to maintain.
   c) setting the power to full.

2. Once the desired speed it attained, _____ should be set at the takeoff or departure setting while establishing a _____ attitude.

3. As the airplane slows to a stall, what must be done with elevator control to maintain the nose-high pitch attitude?

   a) The elevator control must be held rigidly in the stall up position.
   b) The elevator control must be moved progressively further back as the airspeed decreases.
   c) The elevator control must be pushed forward to initiate the stall nose drop.

4. Define the following terms:
   secondary stall _____
   accelerated stall _____

5. The purpose of practicing accelerated stalls is

   a) to learn how they occur and to be able to take prompt recovery action.
   b) to satisfy the PTS whip stall requirement.
   c) to make flight training more dramatic and interesting.

6. A cross-control stall is most apt to occur during

   a) a poorly planned and executed base-to-final approach turn in which the pilot overshoots the centerline of the runway.
   b) descending turns with the power either off or the engine at idle.
   c) airspeed changes in straight-and-level flight.

7. A cross-control stall should only be practiced when safely at altitude because the airplane often stalls with little _____. The nose may pitch down, the inside wing may suddenly _____, and the airplane may continue to roll to an _____ position, or begin a _____.

8. An elevator trim stall shows what can happen if
    a) the trim motor fails in flight.
    b) positive control of the airplane is not maintained during a full-power go-around.
    c) the airplane elevator stalls before main wings.

9. Fill in the blanks to complete some common errors in the performance of intentional stalls.

    • Failure to adequately _____ the area.

    • Inability to recognize an approaching stall condition through the _____ of the airplane.

    • _____ rudder _____.

    • Excessive _____ buildup during recovery.

    • Excessive _____ elevator pressure during recovery resulting in _____ on the wings.

PTS VIII.C – Power-On Stalls

10. Is it acceptable for a private pilot candidate to demonstrate power-on stalls using only 65% of available engine power?
    a) Yes.
    b) No.
    c) Yes, with prior approval from the local Flight Standards District Office.

11. After demonstrating a turning stall, the pilot should recover promptly by simultaneously reducing the angle of attack, increasing power, and
    a) returning the aircraft to the original turn.
    b) retracting any remaining flaps.
    c) leveling the wings to return to a straight-and-level flight attitude.

Answers to Study Questions

1. a

2. power
   climb

3. b

4. a second stall that occurs during the recovery of an earlier stall, when the pilot uses abrupt control movements to try to regain level flight too quickly a stall entered from a higher airspeed when excessive maneuvering loads are imposed on the aircraft

5. a

6. a

7. warning
   drop
   inverted
   spin

8. b

9. clear
   feel
   Inadequate; control
   airspeed
   forward; negative load

10. a

11. c

Spin Awareness

READING ASSIGNMENT
AFH Pages 4-12 to 4-16 – "Spins"
PTS VIII.D – Spin Awareness

Study Questions

AFH Pages 4-12 to 4-16 – "Spins"

? 1. Why does flight training include a thorough discussion of spins and spin recovery?

    a) To familiarize student pilots with flight situations where unintentional spins may occur.
    b) To give students an understanding of the aerodynamic factors related to spins.
    c) To ingrain students with the steps for recovering from unintentional spins.
    d) All of the above.

2. A spin can result from the aircraft being in

    a) an aggravated stall.
    b) nose-low pitch attitude.
    c) descending turn.

3. As an aircraft spirals downward in a spin, the outside wing (rising wing) is

    a) more stalled than the inside wing.
    b) less stalled than the inside wing.
    c) not stalled.

4. A spin is caused when the airplane's wings are stalled and

    a) the airplane is turning
    b) a yawing moment is acting on the airplane.
    c) the airspeed exceeds the design maneuvering speed.

5. During the practice of stall maneuvers, if one wing drops at the beginning of a stall, the correct amount of opposite rudder is very important to

    a) keep the nose from yawing toward the low wing.
    b) initiate a spin in the opposite direction.
    c) maintain level flight.

6. Continued practice of stalls will help the pilot to

    a) develop a more instinctive and prompt reaction in recognizing an approaching spin.
    b) be able to maintain altitude with elevator control throughout the stall.
    c) visualize the nose attitude relative to the horizon at which a stall happens.

7. Determine the phase of a spin as described in each of the following:

_____ The pilot provides the necessary elements for a spin (full stall and yawing moment) either intentionally or accidentally.

_____ The first 4 to 6 seconds in which the spin motion has started but the spin has not yet fully developed.

_____ The angular rotation rate, airspeed, and vertical speed are stabilized and the flightpath is nearly vertical.

_____ The angle of attack of the wing decreases and the stall is broken. The wings regain lift.

8. In a developed spin, if the aircraft is moving, why are the wings still stalled?

   a) The wings are the most stubborn part of the aircraft and don't respond well to the movement of air.
   b) The nearly vertical descent path results in an upward relative wind which increases the angle of attack of the wings beyond the critical angle.
   c) In a developed spin, there is little or no movement of air around the wings to be used for the generation of lift.

9. What is the indication on the airspeed indicator when the aircraft is in a spin?

   a) The airspeed will steadily increase as the airplane descends at a very high rate.
   b) The airspeed will oscillate between V_{NO} and V_{FE}, depending on whether the flaps are extended.
   c) The airspeed will read at or below stall speed.

10. How can you determine if intentional spins are authorized in your aircraft?

    a) The best way is to telephone the aircraft manufacturer and ask.
    b) Limitations would appear in the aircraft's approved AFM/POH.
    c) A warning horn will sound if the aircraft enters a spin.

11. Airplanes placarded against intentional spins are still legally required to be able to recover from a prolonged, fully developed spin in order to obtain a normal category rating.

    a) True.
    b) False.

12. Since recovery from a spin includes recovery from a stalled condition, which aircraft loading condition would make spin recovery difficult or even impossible?

    a) Center of gravity (CG) located significantly forward.
    b) An aft CG.
    c) CG location does not affect aircraft spin characteristics.

13. Two common errors in recovering from spins are excessive back-elevator pressure and insufficient back-elevator pressure. What is the right amount of back-elevator pressure needed?

    a) Enough to cause the stall warning horn to begin to sound momentarily.
    b) Enough to immediately stop the dive and hold altitude.
    c) Enough to avoid excessive airspeed, but not so much as to cause a secondary stall.

Spin Recovery Using the PARENT Method

Don't Make Things Worse	**P**	**Power out**	• Aid in lowering the angle of attack • Reduce left-turning tendencies
	A	**Ailerons neutral**	• Reduce differential angle of attack between wings, which can worsen the spin
Break the Spin	**R**	**Rudder opposite the spin**	• Stop the yawing motion of the airplane
	E	**Elevator down**	• Nose down to break the stall and begin flying again
Recover Smoothly	**N**	**Neutralize rudder**	• Remove any rudder used to stop the spin • Return to straight flight
	T	**Take yourself out of the dive**	• Return smoothly to level flight, without overstressing the aircraft • Do NOT suddenly increase angle of attack or a secondary stall could result • Add power again when level or climbing

FTW-4D

14. What is the first step in spin recovery using the PARENT method?

    a) Nose down, full power.
    b) Full aft elevator.
    c) Power out.

15. In a banked turn, if the pilot attempts to use aileron to roll out of the turn, how does the inside wing's aileron move?

    a) It raises, increasing the angle of attack of that wing.
    b) It lowers, increasing the angle of attack of that wing.
    c) It lowers, decreasing the angle of attack of that wing.

16. Because of the aerodynamics of a spin in which one wing is more stalled than the other, use of ailerons to try to roll out of the spin could

    a) cause the inside wing to become even more stalled than it is.
    b) cause the engine to fail.
    c) result in structural damage to the wing.

17. The correct use of ailerons during a spin is to

    a) bank in the direction opposite the spin.
    b) neutralize the ailerons until the spin and stall are broken and the airplane has returned to normal flight.
    c) feather the ailerons in an attempt to slow the rotation.

18. What flight control does the pilot use to yaw the aircraft (or counteract a yawing motion)?

    a) Yoke.
    b) Throttle.
    c) Rudder pedals.

19. Once the spinning rotation has stopped, why is the elevator pushed down?

    a) To lower the nose and break the stall.
    b) To increase the wing loading and prevent additional yawing.
    c) To improve forward visibility.

20. To stop the yawing motion and recover from a spin, the pilot uses full rudder opposite to the direction of the spin. What is important to remember once the spin and stall are broken?

    _____

    _____

21. Once the spin and stall are broken, the aircraft is likely still descending. How should the pilot take the aircraft out of the dive?

    a) Suddenly and sharply.
    b) As slowly as possible.
    c) Smoothly, without overstressing the aircraft.

PTS VIII.D – Spin Awareness

22. How many intentional spins must be demonstrated by a private pilot candidate taking a FAA Practical Test?

    a) 3.
    b) 1.
    c) 0.

23. What must be demonstrated to the examiner?

    a) Ability to recover from an intentional spin within the first complete turn.
    b) Knowledge of the aerodynamic factors related to spins and procedures for spin recovery.
    c) Ability to enter a spin from a cross-controlled stall on short final approach.

Answers to Study Questions

1. d
2. a
3. b
4. b
5. a
6. a
7. entry phase
   incipient phase
   developed phase
   recovery phase
8. b
9. c
10. b
11. b (false)

12. b
13. c
14. c
15. b
16. a
17. b
18. c
19. a
20. to neutralize the rudder again after the rotation has stopped to remain in straight flight
21. c
22. c
23. b

Takeoffs and Departure Climbs

READING ASSIGNMENT

AFH Pages 5-1 to 5-5 – "General" through "Initial Climb"

AFH Pages 5-7 to 5-8 – "Ground Effect on Takeoff"

PTS II.F – Before Takeoff Check

PTS IV.A – Normal and Crosswind Takeoff and Climb

Study Questions

AFH Pages 5-1 to 5-5 – "General" through "Initial Climb"

1. The takeoff, though relatively simple, often presents

   a) the hardest training challenge for any flight instructor.
   b) the most hazards of any part of a flight.
   c) the fastest propeller speed of any flight condition.

2. The portion of the takeoff procedure during which the airplane is accelerated from a standstill to an airspeed that provides sufficient lift to become airborne is called

   _____

3. When is the initial climb phase normally considered to be complete?

   a) At or above 3,000 feet MSL.
   b) At touchdown on the runway.
   c) When the airplane has reached a safe maneuvering altitude.

4. Part of the standard before takeoff procedures should be

   a) broadcasting your takeoff intentions on 121.50.
   b) ensuring that the engine and all flight controls are operating properly before flight.
   c) shutting down all lights and electrical equipment.

? 5. Why might you see an aircraft do a 360° turn on the ground before taking the runway for takeoff?

   a) The pilot must verify that the aircraft can turn tightly with one wheel completely stopped before beginning flight.
   b) The pilot is trying to delay the takeoff for sequencing.
   c) The pilot is likely visually ensuring that approach and takeoff paths are clear of other aircraft.

6. While taxiing on the runway, the pilot may select ground references aligned with the runway direction as an aid to

    a) maintaining directional control during takeoff.
    b) finding the airport again when returning.
    c) visually compute ground speed on the ground roll.

7. One reason for taking off into the wind (as opposed to with the wind at your back) is to shorten the runway distance required for lift off. The other reason is to

    a) achieve a better rate of climb (higher in a shorter period of time).
    b) reduce wear and stress on the landing gear caused by faster ground speeds.
    c) improve fuel efficiency.

8. How should the throttle be advanced at the start of the takeoff roll?

    a) Smoothly and continuously to takeoff power.
    b) As slowly as possible.
    c) In halfway until rotation speed has been reached, and then full in.

9. To prevent against accidental braking on the takeoff roll, the pilot should check that the toes or balls of both feet are resting on the

    a) floor of the cockpit.
    b) lower portion of the pedals.
    c) upper portion of the pedals.

10. Directional control on the takeoff roll should be maintained with smooth, prompt, positive

    a) aileron movements.
    b) rudder corrections.
    c) bank adjustments.

11. As the aircraft speeds up and approaches lift-off, what is true of the effectiveness of the flight controls?

    a) The flight controls are ineffective on the takeoff roll, but become suddenly effective and necessary for flight at lift-off.
    b) Rudder effectiveness remains constant, with aileron and elevator effectiveness increasing with airspeed.
    c) All of the flight controls gradually become effective to the point where the aircraft is being flown more than taxied.

12. In early stages of takeoff training, flight students may occasionally overcontrol the aircraft when they attempt to control the airplane with control movements instead of

    a) control pressures.
    b) electric rudder and elevator trim.
    c) alignment of the heading indicator to the magnetic compass.

13. An experienced pilot will be able to sense when sufficient airspeed has been acquired for takeoff by
    a) feeling lightly for the resistance in the controls to slight changes in control pressures.
    b) fixating on the airspeed indicator.
    c) calculating the correct takeoff roll distance before the flight and rotating at that point on the runway.

14. When all the flight controls become effective during the takeoff roll in a nosewheel-type airplane, back elevator pressure should be gradually applied to
    a) raise the nosewheel slightly off the runway, thus establishing the takeoff attitude.
    b) force the airplane into the air.
    c) correct for torque and P-factor.

15. The pilot should keep his or her eyes outside the aircraft to maintain
    a) the appropriate nose-up pitch and level bank attitude.
    b) engine RPM within published limits.
    c) eye contact with the pilots of other aircraft.

16. When taking off in gusty wind conditions, the pilot should
    a) force the airplane into the air sooner to prevent wing tips from contacting the ground.
    b) only use as much engine power as would be used to maintain VA in straight and level flight.
    c) allow the airplane to stay on the ground longer to attain an extra margin of speed.

17. On takeoff and climb, when should the pilot retract any flaps that had been extended prior to takeoff?
    a) At lift-off.
    b) Once a V_Y climb attitude has been established.
    c) Once a positive rate of climb has been established.

18. In order to minimize the time spent in the most dangerous portion of an airplane's flight (the takeoff climb before a safe altitude has been reached), it is recommended that the pilot should
    a) hold the nose as high as possible, while keeping the nose of the airplane turned into the wind.
    b) maintain full takeoff power, a V_Y climb attitude, with the wings level and appropriate rudder coordination.
    c) keep the airspeed in the top portions of the green arc.

19. During the climb, the pilot should first make any necessary pitch changes with reference to the natural horizon and hold the new attitude momentarily, and then
    a) return the aircraft to a nose-level, wings-level flight attitude.
    b) glance at the airspeed indicator as a check to see if the new attitude delivers the desired airspeed.
    c) radio the control tower that the plane is "Climb-out complete."

20. After reaching a safe altitude (at least 500 feet or more above the terrain or obstacles), what control and power changes should the pilot make?

    a) The power should be adjusted to the recommended climb setting (if other than full), and the airplane trimmed to relieve the control pressures.
    b) The mixture should be leaned for peak engine efficiency, and forward elevator pressure should be relaxed.
    c) The cross-controlled rudder and aileron should be used to continue in a climbing slip to the left or right.

21. Why is it important for the pilot to maintain a takeoff path that follows the extended runway centerline?

    a) To reduce the need for rudder coordination.
    b) To avoid drifting into obstructions or the path of another aircraft that may be taking off from a parallel runway.
    c) To increase the distance from the airport in case an emergency landing is needed after the loss of one or more engines.

22. Select the answers that make the following statements true.

    The airplane's takeoff performance will be the same / different for a student pilot flying solo than when the student flies with an instructor. Due to the decreased temperature / load , the airplane will become airborne sooner / later and will climb more slowly / rapidly . The pitch problem / attitude that the student has learned to associate with initial climb may also differ due to the decreased weight, and the flight controls may seem more sluggish / sensitive . The solo pilot should be made aware of these differences in advance / after soloing , so they do not create undue tension or a belief that something "abnormal" is occurring.

23. Fill in the blanks to complete some common takeoff and climb errors.

    • Failure to adequately _____ the area prior to taxiing onto the runway.
    • Failure to check _____ instruments for signs of malfunction after applying takeoff power.
    • Failure to anticipate the airplane's _____ on initial power application and acceleration, and correct with appropriate rudder.
    • Relying solely on the _____ rather than the developed feel for indications of speed and airplane controllability during acceleration and lift-off.
    • _____ compensation for torque/P-factor during climb, resulting in a sideslip.
    • "Chasing" the _____, instead of using the airplane's pitch attitude against the horizon to determine a V_Y pitch attitude.

AFH Pages 5-7 to 5-8 – "Ground Effect on Takeoff"

24. Ground effect is most noticeable during takeoff and landing because of the close proximity of the ground, but also because

    a) operating the engine at full throttle further increases the ground effect, especially in low-wing airplanes.
    b) ground effect works by reducing the impact of induced drag, and induced drag is strongest at low airspeeds.
    c) the nose-level flight attitudes at takeoff and landing increase the induced drag.

25. The biggest danger of ground effect to an unsuspecting pilot is in conditions of

    a) high density altitude, high temperature, and/or maximum gross weight.
    b) dense, cold air, at very low aircraft weights.
    c) long, rough surface runways at sea level.

26. In order to safely climb through and beyond ground effect, it is important that the airplane takes off at

    a) the recommended takeoff speed.
    b) V_Y.
    c) the soonest possible moment.

PTS II.F – Before Takeoff Check

27. To what extent should a pilot understand and make use of an appropriate before takeoff checklist?

    a) The pilot should follow the steps by rote, knowing that someone else thought they were important.
    b) Once the pilot knows how to fly, the pilot should know the steps from memory and decide which ones need completion prior to takeoff.
    c) The pilot should make consistent use of the before takeoff checklist, know the reasons for checking each item and how to detect malfunctions.

?

28. The PTS says that pilots must divide their attention inside and outside the cockpit. What are some things that you think a pilot should look for inside and outside the cockpit prior to takeoff?

Things INSIDE the Cockpit	Things OUTSIDE the Cockpit
1) _____	1) _____
2) _____	2) _____
3) _____	3) _____

29. Just prior to taking off, a pilot should review takeoff performance _____, takeoff distances, the planned departure, and _____ procedures

PTS IV.A – Normal and Crosswind Takeoff and Climb

30. At the start of the takeoff roll for takeoff and climb demonstrations on the FAA Practical Test, a private pilot candidate is evaluated on whether he or she positions the flight controls correctly for the

    _____

31. At lift-off of a normal or crosswind takeoff, what airspeeds will the designated FAA examiner expect the pilot to attain to demonstrate proper control of the aircraft?

    a) V_Y at lift-off, then cruise climb after reaching 50 feet.
    b) V_X at lift-off, then maintain a climbing VA pitch and bank attitude.
    c) Lift off at the recommended airspeed and accelerate to V_Y.

32. When must proper wind-drift correction be maintained?

    a) After reaching a safe maneuvering altitude.
    b) When the aircraft is first established in the climb.
    c) Throughout the takeoff and climb.

Answers to Study Questions

1. b
2. takeoff roll (or ground roll)
3. c
4. b
5. c
6. a
7. b
8. a
9. b
10. b
11. c
12. a
13. a
14. a
15. a
16. c
17. c
18. b
19. b
20. a
21. b
22. different
    load
    sooner
    rapidly
    attitude
    sensitive
    in advance

23. clear
    engine
    left-turning tendency
    airspeed indicator
    Inadequate
    airspeed indicator
24. b
25. a
26. a
27. c
28. Inside: mixture, flap settings, yoke position,
              engine oil temperature/pressure gauges,
              lights as needed, transponder on
    Outside: approach and departure path clear,
              other aircraft on taxiways, wind
              indicators, taxiway and runway
              centerlines, flight control surfaces
29. airspeeds
    emergency
30. current wind conditions
31. c
32. c

Crosswind Takeoffs

READING ASSIGNMENT
AFH Pages 5-5 to 5-7 – "Crosswind Takeoff"

Study Questions

1. The technique for taking off with a crosswind

   a) closely parallels the crosswind correction technique used in taxiing.
   b) is the same as for taking off in an emergency high-performance climb situation.
   c) is to use full rudder application on the side from which the wind is blowing.

2. At the start of a crosswind takeoff, how much aileron correction is used into the wind?

   a) No aileron, because wings are level.
   b) Full aileron.
   c) As much aileron as the pilot estimates will be required at lift-off.

3. On the takeoff ground roll with a crosswind, the airplane is held to the centerline of the runway with

   a) ailerons.
   b) rudder/nosewheel steering.
   c) elevator.

4. What is the correct amount of rudder/nosewheel steering control to be applied during the ground roll?

   _____
   _____
   _____

5. During the takeoff roll, as ailerons become more effective and the crosswind component of the relative wind becomes less effective, the pilot should

   a) hold firm to the full aileron deflection until a safe altitude above the ground (usually 500 r 600 feet AGL).
   b) attempt to raise the upwind wing first to prevent skipping.
   c) gradually reduce the aileron pressures to just the amount required to keep the plane from skipping the left or right.

Crosswind Takeoffs

6. In a well-executed takeoff with a crosswind, the downwind wing should lift off the runway first with airplane continuing the remainder of the takeoff roll on the upwind wheel alone.

    a) True.
    b) False.

7. If proper crosswind correction is being applied, as soon as the airplane is airborne from a crosswind takeoff, it will be _____ into the wind sufficiently to counteract the drifting effect of the wind.

8. Once a positive rate of climb has been established and the airplane is beyond the point that the airplane could safely set back down on the runway, the airplane should be

    a) flown at V_{FE} until the flaps have been extended.
    b) turned into the wind and the wings rolled level.
    c) reduced to a level pitch attitude and airspeed increased to the desired cruise airspeed.

9. Unless otherwise instructed by ATC, a VFR pilot established in the climb in a crosswind situation should fly the aircraft in such a way as to

    a) maintain a constant ground track, using the runway centerline.
    b) maintain a constant heading, using the runway heading.
    c) point the aircraft nose directly into the wind.

10. Which of the following are common errors in the performance of crosswind takeoffs?
(Check all that apply.)

    ☐ Failure to keep the control yoke fixed and unmoving throughout the takeoff roll.
    ☐ Mechanical use of aileron control rather than sensing the need for varying aileron control input through feel for the airplane.
    ☐ Excessive aileron input in the latter stage of the takeoff roll resulting in a steep bank into the wind at lift-off.
    ☐ Inadequate drift correction after lift-off, resulting in the aircraft path deviating to one side or the other of the extended runway centerline.

Answers to Study Questions

1. a
2. b
3. b
4. whatever rudder pressure is required to keep the airplane rolling straight down the runway
5. c
6. a (true)
7. sideslipping
8. b
9. a

10. ☐ Failure to keep the control yoke fixed and unmoving throughout the takeoff roll
☒ Mechanical use of aileron control rather than sensing the need for varying aileron control input through feel for the airplane
☒ Excessive aileron input in the latter stage of the takeoff roll resulting in a steep bank into the wind at lift-off
☒ Inadequate drift correction after lift-off, resulting in the aircraft path deviating to one side or the other of the extended runway centerline

FTW-5B

Short-Field Takeoff

READING ASSIGNMENT
AFH Pages 5-8 to 5-10 – "Short-Field Takeoff and Maximum Performance Climb"
PTS IV.E – Short-Field Takeoff and Maximum Performance Climb

Study Questions

AFH Pages 5-8 to 5-10 – "Short-Field Takeoff and Maximum Performance Climb"

1. Short-field operations refer to takeoff and landing operations at fields with either very short runways, or where the available takeoff area is

   a) restricted by obstructions.
   b) longer than 1,600 feet.
   c) at elevations above 4,000 feet MSL.

2. To takeoff from a short field requires the pilot to operate the airplane

   a) beyond the capabilities described in the airplane POH.
   b) at the limit of its takeoff performance capability.
   c) in the same way as on normal length runways.

3. The two goals for a short-field takeoff and climb are to operate the aircraft so as to achieve the shortest
   _____ and the steepest _____.

4. What resource specifies the correct power setting, flap setting, and airspeeds that should be used for a short-field takeoff and climb?

   a) The FAA's Pilot's Handbook of Aeronautical Knowledge.
   b) The FAA's Aeronautical Information Manual.
   c) The manufacturer's FAA-approved Airplane Flight Manual or Pilot's Operating Handbook.

5. The airspeed V_X provides the greatest gain in _____ for a given _____ over the ground.

6. The airspeed V_Y provides the greatest gain in altitude

   a) in the shortest amount of time.
   b) at the fastest airspeed.
   c) longest distance.

7. Precise control of airspeed in a short-field takeoff and maximum performance climb is critical because

   a) in some airplanes, a deviation of even 5 knots can significantly decrease climb performance and increase the risk of contact with ground obstructions.
   b) the engine can stall if climb speeds are not carefully maintained.
   c) the center of gravity can shift dangerously aft during a climb.

8. What is especially critical at the start of the takeoff roll for a short-field takeoff?

   a) The airplane is rolled continuously onto the runway centerline with minimal braking.
   b) The airplane is positioned at the very beginning of the takeoff area to ensure maximum use of available runway distance.
   c) A takeoff clearance is not required for short-field takeoffs even at tower-controlled airports.

9. If the aircraft manufacturer specifies that flaps should be used during a short-field takeoff, when should the pilot extend the flaps to the recommended setting?

   a) Prior to beginning the takeoff.
   b) As the aircraft accelerates down the runway.
   c) Once the aircraft has cleared the final obstacle and can climb freely.

10. Which of the following is NOT a recommended procedure for the ground roll of a short-field takeoff?

    a) Power should be applied smoothly and without hesitation to accelerate the aircraft as rapidly as possible.
    b) Directional control is primarily maintained through the use of differential braking.
    c) As the takeoff roll progresses, the airplane's pitch attitude and angle of attack should be adjusted to that which results in the minimum amount of drag.

11. Unless otherwise specified by the manufacturer, what speed should the pilot rotate at and maintain until obstacles are cleared?

    a) V_{S1}.
    b) V_X.
    c) V_Y.

12. On climb out, once the aircraft has cleared any obstacles (or has reached an altitude of at least 50 feet if no obstacles are involved), the pilot should

    a) reduce engine power and lean the mixture for the final cruise altitude.
    b) increase the nose attitude and continue the climb at minimum controllable airspeed.
    c) decrease the pitch attitude slightly, maintain V_Y and retract any flaps used during the takeoff.

13. During a short-field takeoff and maximum performance climb, the pilot's eyes should be

    a) on the engine tachometer to watch for any signs of engine trouble.
    b) glued to the airspeed indicator.
    c) outside the aircraft watching for obstacles, maintaining pitch attitude using the horizon as reference, with occasional quick peeks inside to verify airspeed.

14. As a general rule, if flaps are to be retracted during a climb, it should be done

    a) in stages, to avoid sudden loss of lift.
    b) as quickly as possible.
    c) before reaching 100 feet AGL.

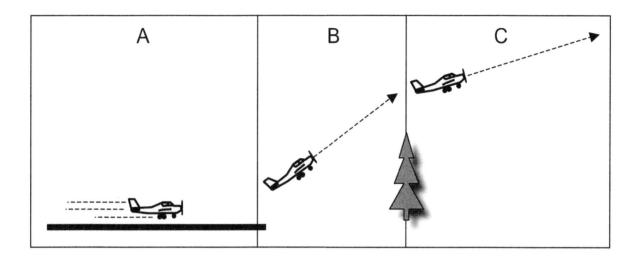

15. Use the diagram above to identify in which phase of a short-field takeoff and climb the following items apply. (Check all that apply.)

Maintain V_Y	☐ A	☐ B	☐ C
Maintain V_X	☐ A	☐ B	☐ C
Minimal braking	☐ A	☐ B	☐ C
Eyes primarily outside the cockpit	☐ A	☐ B	☐ C
Retract flaps (if used)	☐ A	☐ B	☐ C
Manage pitch to keep drag at a minimum	☐ A	☐ B	☐ C

PTS IV.E – Short-Field Takeoff and Maximum Performance Climb

16. As with any other takeoff, at the start of a short-field takeoff the flight controls should be positioned

    a) with yoke handles even and hands resting comfortably in the pilot's lap.
    b) down and away from the wind.
    c) appropriately for the current wind conditions.

17. For a short-field takeoff, the aircraft should be positioned to utilize the _____ available takeoff area, with the aircraft aligned with the runway _____.

18. If appropriate, the pilot should apply full brakes to keep the aircraft from moving until

    a) full takeoff power has been applied and verified on the engine tachometer.
    b) the tower issues a "ground roll" clearance.
    c) V_X has been reached.

19. What is the PTS performance standard for maintaining airspeed during the climb to clear the obstacle in a short-field takeoff and maximum performance climb?

_____

Answers to Study Questions

1. a
2. b
3. ground roll
   angle of climb
4. c
5. altitude
   distance
6. a
7. a
8. b
9. a
10. b
11. b
12. c

13. c
14. a
15. Maintain V_Y ☐ A ☐ B ☒ C
    Maintain V_X ☐ A ☒ B ☐ C
    Minimal braking   ☒ A ☐ B ☐ C
    Eyes primarily outside
    the cockpit   ☒ A ☒ B ☒ C
    Retract flaps (if used)   ☐ A ☐ B ☒ C
    Manage pitch to keep
    drag at a minimum   ☒ A ☐ B ☐ C
16. c
17. maximum
    centerline
18. a
19. +10/-5 knots

Soft-Field Takeoff

READING ASSIGNMENT
AFH Pages 5-10 to 5-11 – "Soft/Rough-Field Takeoff and Climb"
PTS IV.C – Soft-Field Takeoff and Climb

Study Questions

AFH Pages 5-10 to 5-11 – "Soft/Rough-Field Takeoff and Climb"

1. Which of the following is the best reason for why special takeoff techniques are used for taking off from a soft field?

   a) Normal takeoff procedures could result in mud or dirt being flung up onto the wings or fuselage dirtying the airplane.

   b) Getting airborne as quickly as possible is the best way to eliminate the drag caused by tall grass, soft sand, mud, or snow.

   c) Landing gear tends to float or skid along the top surface of grass landing strips, causing the aircraft to become airborne sooner than expected.

 2. If normal takeoff procedures were employed on the take off roll at an airport with an extremely soft runway surface, the airplane's acceleration may be reduced to the point that

   a) adequate takeoff speed might not be attained even after using the full available runway length.

   b) additional fuel is required to complete the flight.

   c) the pilot may have to use full throttle for takeoff.

3. Soft or rough fields are also a concern because on the ground roll landing gear can become

   a) stuck, causing possible damage to landing gear or causing the aircraft to tip over.

   b) wet or caked in mud, reducing aerodynamic efficiency to the point of stalling the aircraft.

   c) airborne before the rest of the aircraft.

4. Soft-field takeoff procedures are quite different from those used for short fields with firm, smooth surfaces.

   a) True.

   b) False.

5. To minimize the hazards associated with soft or rough runways, support of the airplane's weight

   a) must be transferred from the wheels to the wings as rapidly as possible during the takeoff roll.

   b) should be increased with additional structural bracing on the landing gear struts.

   c) must remain on the main landing gear as long as possible.

6. Which of the following are appropriate ways that additional lift can be created sooner on the takeoff roll from a soft field? (Check all that apply.)

   ☐ Establishing and maintaining a nose-high pitch attitude as early as possible
   ☐ Maintaining forward pressure on the control yoke to keep the aircraft on the runway
   ☐ Using partial flaps (if specified by the airplane manufacturer)
   ☐ Use differential braking (rather than rudder) for directional control
   ☐ Flying without the normal VFR fuel reserve

★ 7. While taxiing on a soft surface, which of the following methods decrease the risk of the aircraft from becoming bogged down or stuck, and which increase the risk?

	Risk of Aircraft Becoming Stuck	
	Decreases	**Increases**
Minimal or no braking	☐	☐
Maintaining some engine power	☐	☐
Taxiing slowly with frequent stops	☐	☐
Full back pressure on the control yoke	☐	☐
Tight, sharp turns	☐	☐

8. How is ground effect used to the pilot's advantage during a soft-field takeoff?

   a) Ground effect is used to keep pressure on the wheels during the takeoff roll for improved directional control.
   b) Ground effect allows the aircraft to lift off the runway early, so that it can be accelerated in the air without the drag caused by contact with the surface.
   c) The power output of the engine is increased while operating in ground effect, allowing for additional takeoff power.

9. While executing a soft-field takeoff and climb in an airplane for which the manufacturer has specified use of flaps, when would the flaps be extended and retracted?

   a) Extended once wheels have lifted off the runway, and retracted at cruise altitude.
   b) Extended prior to beginning takeoff, and retracted once aloft in ground effect.
   c) Extended prior to beginning takeoff, and retracted once established on a V_X or V_Y climb.

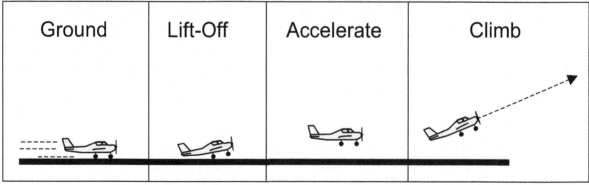

10. Draw lines to connect each phase of a soft-field takeoff with the appropriate pitch control input.

Ground Roll ▶   ◀ Aft control pressure relaxing to transition to level flight
Lift-Off ▶   ◀ Pitch up for target airspeed
Accelerate ▶   ◀ Full aft controls until nose is raised to desired attitude
Climb ▶   ◀ Increasing forward control pressure required to maintain desired altitude

11. In a soft-field takeoff, the airplane will become airborne at an airspeed slower than a safe climb speed.

    a) True.
    b) False.

12. The aircraft is most at risk of settling back to the surface if the pilot

    a) initiates the climb before achieving sufficient airspeed, or attempts to climb too steeply.
    b) allows too much airspeed to build up during lift-off or acceleration in ground effect.
    c) maintains positive control of the pitch attitude throughout takeoff.

13. A common error for pilots performing a soft-field takeoff is

    a) waiting too long to begin the climb.
    b) allowing the wheels to air dry too long before retracting the landing gear, after taking off from a wet field.
    c) using abrupt and/or excessive elevator control while attempting to level off in ground effect.

PTS IV.C – Soft-Field Takeoff and Climb

14. Prior to takeoff from a soft field, the pilot should clear the area and taxi onto the takeoff surface at a speed consistent with safety without _____.

15. On the ground roll, weight should be transferred from the wheels to the wings

    a) as rapidly as possible.
    b) after reaching the appropriate rotation speed.
    c) by retracting the flaps.

16. The airplane should remain in ground effect while accelerating until _____ or _____.

17. As with any other takeoff and climb, once established in the climb, the pilot should

    a) accelerate to cruise speed.
    b) pull throttle back to idle.
    c) complete the appropriate climb checklist.

FTW-5D

Answers to Study Questions

1. b

2. a

3. a

4. a (true)

5. a

---

6. ☒ Establishing and maintaining a nose-high pitch attitude as early as possible
    ☐ Maintaining forward pressure on the control yoke to keep the aircraft on the runway
    ☒ Using partial flaps (if specified by the airplane manufacturer)
    ☐ Use differential braking (rather than rudder) for directional control
    ☐ Flying without the normal VFR fuel reserve

7.
	Decreases risk	Increases risk
Minimal or no braking	☒	☐
Maintaining some engine power	☒	☐
Taxiing slowly with frequent stops	☐	☒
Full back pressure on the control yoke	☒	☐
Tight, sharp turns	☐	☒

8. b

9. c

10. Ground Roll ▶ — Aft control pressure relaxing to transition to level flight
    Lift-Off ▶ — Pitch for target airspeed
    Accelerate ▶ — Full aft controls
    Climb ▶ — Increasing forward control pressure required to maintain desired altitude

---

11. a (true)

12. a

13. c

14. stopping

15. a

16. V_X or V_Y

17. c

Ground Reference Maneuvers

READING ASSIGNMENT
AFH Pages 6-1 to 6-9 – "Purpose and Scope" through "Turns Around a Point"
PTS VI – Ground Reference Maneuvers

Study Questions

AFH Pages 6-1 to 6-9 – "Purpose and Scope" through "Turns Around a Point"

1. Flight training low to the ground using nearby ground objects as reference points is noticeably different from high altitude training using distance reference points in at least one key way. What is it?

    a) Operations close to the ground require great engine power settings.
    b) Operations close to the ground force the pilot to analyze and factor in the effects of wind on the airplane's intended ground course.
    c) At low altitudes, flight control surfaces are less effective and controls are sluggish.

2. One reason that student pilots begin flight training in ground reference maneuvers as soon as they show proficiency in the fundamental flight maneuvers is

    a) to begin to develop a habit of dividing attention inside and outside of the airplane.
    b) to keep more of the flight training closer to the ground where it is safer.
    c) to allow students to fly over their houses and wave to their friends.

3. Ground reference maneuvers are performed at relatively low altitudes while applying _____ as needed to follow a predetermined track or path over the ground.

4. Intentionally pointing the nose of the airplane in a slightly different direction than the actual course you intend to fly over the ground is called

    a) archetypal adjustment.
    b) wind correction.
    c) radial dihedral.

5. At what altitude should ground reference maneuvers be flown?

    a) At or below 500 above the ground (AGL)
    b) At approximately 600 to 1,000 feet AGL.
    c) At or above 3,000 feet AGL.

6. Due to the altitude at which these maneuvers are performed, both the instructor and student should be alert for

   a) available forced-landing fields in the event the need arises.
   b) commercial IFR air traffic.
   c) double-deck buses and trucks with antennae that extend over 20 feet vertically.

 7. To demonstrate your understanding of wind correction, imagine that you are aboard a satellite looking down on the earth and taking snapshots of an airplane as it flies along a course on the ground. In the diagram on the left, the pilot is not applying any wind correction. Show the airplane's location and heading every few seconds. In the diagram on the right, show the same for an airplane in which the pilot was using the correct wind correction.

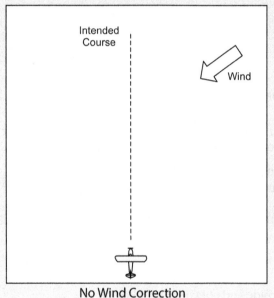

No Wind Correction

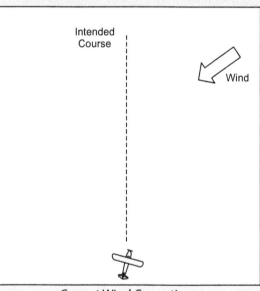

Correct Wind Correction

8. Wind correction is required only when trying to maintain a course on the ground that is in a straight line, and is not required to fly a circular ground track.

   a) True.
   b) False.

9. Select the answers that make the following statement true.

   Groundspeed differs from airspeed in several ways. In flight, <u>airspeed / groundspeed</u> tends to remain constant for any combination of attitude, <u>power setting / fuel capacity</u> , and configuration. For example, in a well-executed, level 360° turn, the airspeed should change <u>constantly / very little</u> .

   On the contrary, <u>airspeed / groundspeed</u> is constantly changing, reacting to changes in <u>humidity / wind strength</u> and the <u>altitude / angle</u> from which the wind is blowing relative to the <u>service ceiling / flight direction</u> of the airplane. In a well-executed, level 360° turn in windy conditions, the airspeed should change <u>constantly / very little</u> while the groundspeed changes <u>constantly / very little</u> .

10. Whenever the airplane is headed into the wind, groundspeed is

    a) increased.
    b) decreased.
    c) unaffected.

 11. While flying a circular course over the ground, at the places in the turn that groundspeed is high the angle of bank must be

    a) increased to hold the airplane over the turning course.
    b) decreased to factor in the faster groundspeed.
    c) increased when climbing, and decreased when descending.

12. How does wind affect a 180° ground reference turn made using a constant bank angle?

    a) The wind will distort the shape of the turn, unless other corrections are made.
    b) The various opposing effects of the wind cancel out over the 180° and the turn will be unaffected.
    c) The wind will always slow the groundspeed and reduce the turning radius.

13. The rectangular course is a training maneuver in which the ground track of the airplane is

    _____ from all sides of a selected rectangular area on the ground.

14. While flying the rectangular course, the altitude and airspeed should

    a) be held constant.
    b) fluctuate depending on the relative direction of the wind.
    c) increase during the downwind legs of the course.

 15. The diagram below shows a student pilot practice-flying a rectangular course with wind coming from the north. To demonstrate your understanding of the influence of the wind, draw the course that would result if the novice pilot did NOT use any wind correction while flying the course.

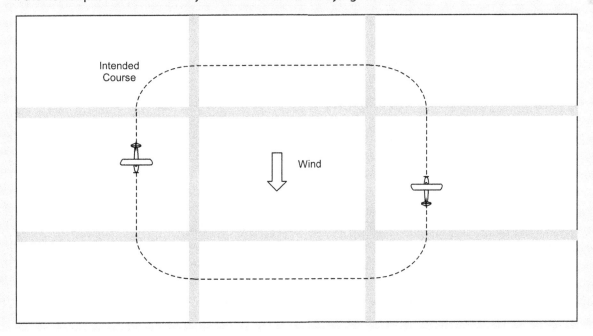

FTW-6

Ground Reference Maneuvers

16. When the wind direction is not parallel to any side of the rectangular course, the pilot will need to use wind correction on all four sides. In the diagram below, draw the airplane on each leg of the course and show the approximate wind correction the pilot will need on each side of the course.

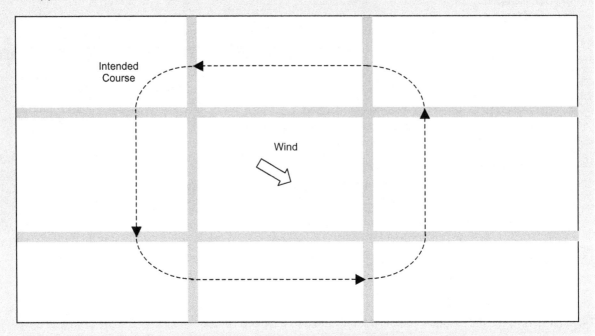

17. In a no wind situation, the heading of the airplane turns exactly 90° at each corner of the rectangular course. However, when wind correction is used the heading change at each corner will be larger or smaller than 90°.

On each leg of the rectangular course in the diagram below, draw the airplane, show the approximate wind correction required, and determine whether the heading change in each corner is larger or smaller than 90°.

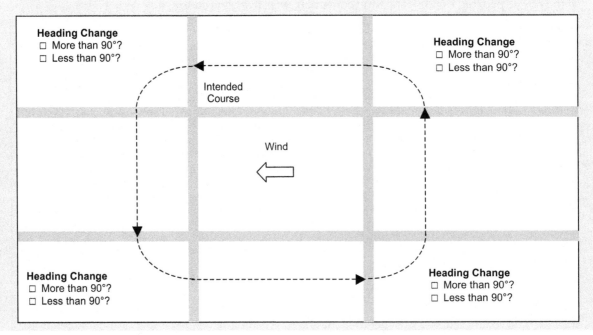

18. Although the amount of turn may vary in each corner of the rectangular pattern, the space available in which to complete the turn

    a) changes accordingly.
    b) remains the same.
    c) changes with groundspeed.

19. For the airplane to complete a larger change in heading in the same amount of space, the pilot needs to

    a) increase the bank angle.
    b) decrease the bank angle.
    c) keep the bank angle the same on all corners of the rectangular course.

20. Although the airspeed should remain the same throughout the maneuver, how does the groundspeed vary?

    a) The groundspeed is highest in the crosswind legs.
    b) The groundspeed is highest whenever the wind is coming from behind the airplane.
    c) The groundspeed is highest when the nose is pointed approximately into the wind.

21. As the pilot approaches the corner while flying a rectangular course, what should the pilot be thinking about in preparation for the turn? (Check all that apply.)

    ☐ Comparing the wind correction required after the turn with the wind correction on the current leg (to determine amount of turn required)
    ☐ Estimating the effects of pressure altitude on pitch trim performance
    ☐ Visualizing the airplane's path along the next leg of the rectangular course equidistant from the ground reference line
    ☐ Using the natural horizon as an aid to maintaining a level turn
    ☐ Reviewing the direction of the wind and estimating the steepness of bank angle required to complete the turn in the space available

22. Fill in the blanks to indicate some of the common errors in the performance of rectangular courses.

    • Failure to adequately _____ the area.
    • Failure to establish the appropriate _____ angle resulting in the airplane drifting off the desired course legs.
    • Gaining or _____ altitude.
    • Poor rudder/aileron _____ resulting in slipping or skidding in turns.
    • Inadequate visual attention outside of the aircraft looking out for _____.

23. The goal in performing S-turns across a road is to have

    a) a flight path over the ground of semicircles of equal size.
    b) the time in flight for each half circle to be equal.
    c) the altitude and groundspeed to remain constant throughout.

Ground Reference Maneuvers

24. Why is the wind correction required in performing an S-turn across a road more advanced than the wind correction required in flying a rectangular course?

    a) The pilot must use both inside and outside references to determine the size of the semicircles.
    b) The airplane must turn with steeper bank angles in flying an S-turn.
    c) Since ground speed is constantly changing, the pilot must continually adjust bank angle to compensate.

25. What is the appropriate way to enter an S-turn across a road?

    a) With wings parallel to the road and the nose pointed into the wind.
    b) From the upwind side, at the selected altitude on a downwind heading.
    c) At an altitude of at least 3,000 feet AGL.

26. As in most ground reference maneuvers, when is the required bank angle in a turn the greatest?

    a) When the wind is from behind and groundspeed is highest.
    b) With wings parallel to the road and the nose pointed into the wind.
    c) When flying headings into the wind.

 27. How should the airplane be positioned when crossing the road?

    a) The wings should be at a shallow bank angle with the nose slightly below the horizon.
    b) Wings level and parallel to the road.
    c) Upwind wingtip slightly forward of the road, and downwind wingtip slightly behind the road.

28. Without the proper wind correction, which semicircle will tend to be larger?

    a) The semicircular path upwind of the road.
    b) The semicircular path downwind of the road.
    c) Wind does not tend to influence the size of the semicircles.

 29. If in approaching and crossing the road the inside wing crosses the road before the outside wing, what mistake has the pilot made?

    a) The airspeed was not increased enough to make up for the decrease in groundspeed into the wind.
    b) The angle of bank used was not sufficient to complete the turn before crossing the road.
    c) Incorrect rudder coordination has resulted in a skidding turn.

30. One of the biggest errors pilots make in performance of S-turns across a road is the inability to visualize the

    _____.

? 31. The goal of the ground reference maneuver, turns around a point, is to maintain a constant bank angle, with the wingtip locked on the ground reference point.

    a) True.
    b) False.

66

32. Select the answers that make the following statement true.

> If a turn around a point is completed correctly, the radius of the circular ground track will change constantly / remain fixed as the airplane completes the circuit, and the angle of bank should change constantly / remain fixed . If wind is present, the pilot will experience a changing airspeed / groundspeed throughout the maneuver.

33. While flying the downwind arc in a turn around a point, why might a beginning pilot tend to skid the turn?
   a) The pilot may attempt to use excessive rudder to make up for an insufficient bank angle and hold the intended ground track in the turn.
   b) The pilot may have overbanked the airplane at the start of the turn.
   c) Left-turning tendencies are greatest at high groundspeeds.

34. During the performance of a turn around a point, what should the pilot be looking for outside of the cockpit?
   a) The reference point at the center of the turn.
   b) Wingtip position relative to the horizon.
   c) The desired ground track, the horizon for pitch/bank reference, and for other aircraft.

35. During the performance of a turn around a point, what should the pilot be looking for inside the cockpit?
   a) A constant distance from the reference point (using GPS or other distance measuring equipment).
   b) Occasional quick glances at the altimeter and turn coordinator.
   c) Close monitoring of the altimeter to detect any tiny change in altitude.

PTS VI – Ground Reference Maneuvers

36. What are the ground reference maneuver performance standards with regard to altitude?

Entry altitude: _____

Maintaining altitude: _____

37. How is the pilot's attention evaluated?
   a) The pilot must pay attention to whatever the examiner is saying during the flight.
   b) The pilot must divide attention between airplane control and the ground track while maintaining coordinated flight.
   c) 90% of the maneuver must be performed with the pilot's attention outside the aircraft.

38. In the performance of ground reference maneuvers, the pilot must maintain the airplane's airspeed ±_____ knots.

39. How should the pilot plan to enter the rectangular course?
   a) 45° to the downwind leg.
   b) Crosswind, abeam the downwind corner.
   c) In any manner.

FTW-6

Answers to Study Questions

1. b

2. a

3. wind drift correction

4. b

5. b

6. a

7.

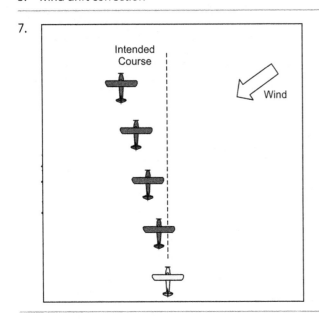
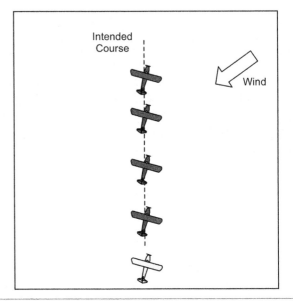

8. b (false)

9. airspeed
   power setting
   very little
   groundspeed
   wind strength
   angle
   flight direction
   very little
   constantly

10. b

11. a

12. a

13. equidistant

14. a

Answers to Study Questions

15.

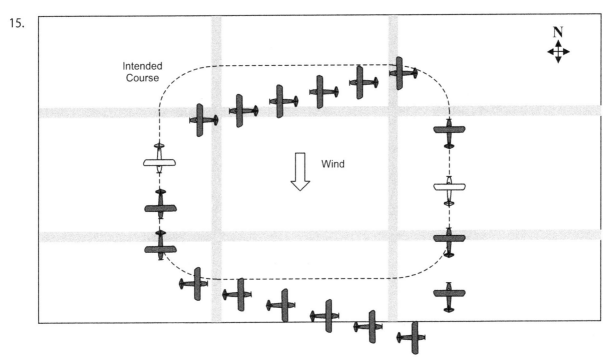

16.

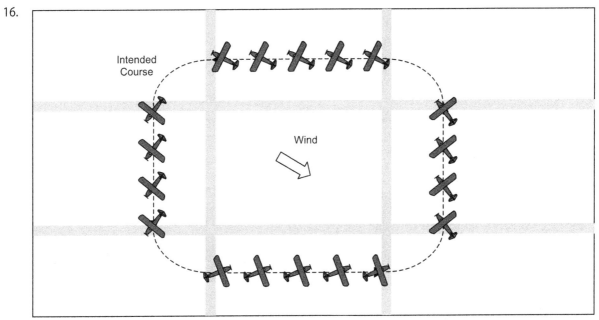

Answers to Study Questions

17.

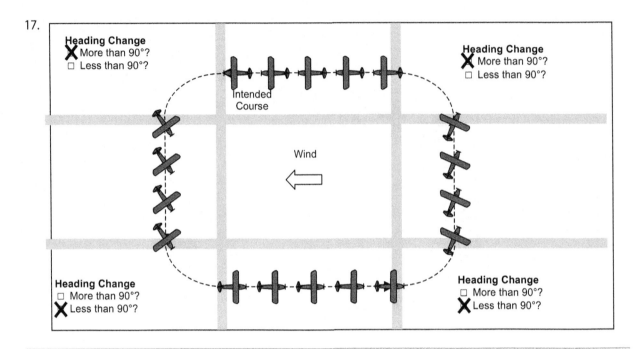

18. b

19. a

20. b

21. ☒ Comparing the wind correction required after the turn with the wind correction on the current leg (to determine amount of turn required)

☐ Estimating the effects of pressure altitude on pitch trim performance

☒ Visualizing the airplane's path along the next leg of the rectangular course equidistant from the ground reference line

☒ Using the natural horizon as an aid to maintaining a level turn

☒ Reviewing the direction of the wind and estimating the steepness of bank angle required to complete the turn in the space available

22. clear
wind correction
losing
coordination
other aircraft

23. a

24. c

25. b

26. a

27. b

28. b

29. b

30. half circle ground track

31. b (false)

32. remain fixed
change constantly
groundspeed

33. a

34. c

35. b

36. 600 feet to 1,000 feet AGL
±100 feet

37. b

38. 10

39. a

Airport Traffic Patterns

READING ASSIGNMENT

AFH Chapter 7 – *Airport Traffic Patterns*

Study Questions

1. Airport traffic patterns provide specific routes for

   a) arriving aircraft, but departures are at the discretion of the pilot in command.
   b) takeoffs, departures, arrivals, and landings.
   c) cross-country flights over long distances using radio navigation equipment.

2. Airport operating rules and procedures are based not only on logic or common sense, but also on courtesy, and their objective is

   a) to separate VFR traffic from IFR traffic.
   b) minimize the time an aircraft spends in the air.
   c) to keep air traffic moving with maximum safety and efficiency.

3. At airports with operating control towers, the tower operator may instruct pilots

   a) to enter the traffic pattern at any point, or to make a straight-in approach without flying the usual traffic pattern.
   b) to stop in mid-air to give way to conflicting traffic.
   c) to negotiate with other departing or landing traffic about how to share the runway.

 4. On the blank lines in the diagram below, identify the legs of a standard airport traffic pattern.

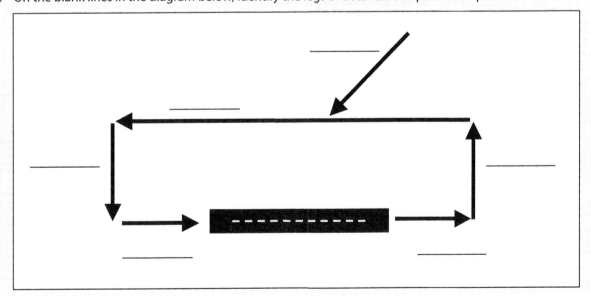

5. When landing at an airport without a control tower, and with no apparent other air traffic in the pattern, how can the pilot determine which runway and traffic pattern to use?

    a) Pick the largest runway and make all turns to the left.
    b) Overfly the airport and observe wind and traffic pattern indicators on the ground.
    c) Radio a flight service station and request clearance to land.

6. After flying over the uncontrolled airport and determining the proper pattern direction, what should the pilot do to reach the correct pattern altitude?

    a) Proceed to a point well clear of the pattern before descending to the pattern altitude.
    b) Make a descending entry into the downwind leg before turning to base and final.
    c) Adjust the descent rate to allow the airplane to maintain a stabilized descent all the way through to landing.

7. How should the traffic pattern be entered when approaching an airport for landing?

    a) The pilot should align the airplane with the runway of intended use as far out as possible.
    b) On a 45° angle to the downwind leg, headed toward a point abeam the midpoint of the runway to be used for landing.
    c) At an altitude at least 2,000 feet above the runway until aligned with the runway on final approach.

8. How long should the entry leg of the traffic pattern be?

    a) 2 to 5 statute miles.
    b) ½ to 1 mile.
    c) Long enough to provide a clear view of the entire traffic pattern, and to allow the pilot time to plan the intended path in the pattern and the landing approach.

9. Where is the downwind leg of the traffic pattern in relation to the runway?

    a) Perpendicular to the runway at a point approximately 45° from the approach end of the runway.
    b) ½ to 1 mile out from the landing runway, with the distance gradually varying as a result of any crosswind influence.
    c) Parallel to the runway about ½ to 1 mile out.

 10. Which is the true statement regarding flight in an airport traffic pattern?

    a) The airplane heading is the most critical determining factor. Headings should be selected that are on the same magnetic direction as the landing runway, and at 90°, 180°, and 270°.
    b) The traffic pattern is a ground reference maneuver and the airplane's heading should be adjusted as required to correct for wind drift and to keep the ground track in a rectangular pattern aligned with the runway.
    c) Once the airplane is on crosswind and downwind the ground track is held constant, but on base and final the pilot transitions to keeping the airplane's heading aligned tightly with the runway's magnetic direction.

Answers to Study Questions

1. b

2. c

3. a

4.

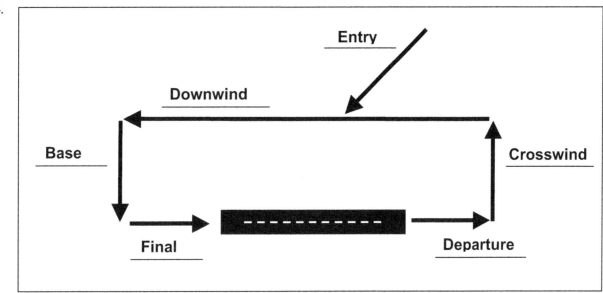

5. b

6. a

7. b

8. c

9. c

10. b

Airport Procedures

READING ASSIGNMENT

Aeronautical Information Manual (AIM)

AIM §4-3-1 – General
AIM §4-3-2 – Airports with an
　　　　Operating Control Tower
AIM §4-3-3 – Traffic Patterns
AIM §4-3-5 – Unexpected Maneuvers in
　　　　the Airport Traffic Pattern
AIM §4-3-6 – Use of Runways/Declared
　　　　Distances
AIM §4-3-12 – Low Approach

AIM §4-3-14 – Communications
AIM §4-3-18 – Taxiing
AIM §4-3-20 – Exiting the Runway
　　　　after Landing
AIM §4-3-22 – Option Approach
AIM §4-3-23 – Use of Aircraft Lights
AIM §4-4-1 – ATC clearance
AIM §4-4-13 – Runway separation
AIM §4-4-14 – Visual separation

Study Questions

AIM §4-3-1 – General

1. Why does the potential for in-flight accidents increase near airports?

   a) Airport flight rules are confusing and often encourage reckless and unsafe behavior.
   b) Aircraft are often in climb or descent attitudes that limit forward visibility, and pilots are occupied with cockpit duties associated with climb management or landing preparation.
   c) Tower controllers often put airplanes in closer proximity than the pilots can safely handle.

AIM §4-3-2 – Airports with an Operating Control Tower

2. When intending to approach and land at an airport with an operating control tower, how far out from the airport should the initial radio callup to the tower be made?

   a) 4 nautical miles.
   b) 8 nautical miles.
   c) 15 nautical miles.

3. Once outside the surface area of a Class B, Class C, or Class D airspace, what must a pilot receive before changing from the tower radio frequency?

   a) Nothing.
   b) Clearance to change frequency.
   c) Clearance to exit the airspace.

4. The term "upwind leg" has been adopted by pilots and control towers and means

   a) The same thing as the "departure leg."
   b) A leg parallel to the runway and in the direction of landing but offset to one side, used for executing a go around.
   c) Any leg in which the aircraft is exhibiting a positive rate of climb.

5. What general rule applies to the length of the departure leg before the pilots turns crosswind?

    a) The airplane must be above 300 feet AGL and within ½ mile from the departure end of the runway.
    b) The airplane must be at least ½ mile from the departure end of the runway and at least 300 feet AGL.
    c) The airplane must be at least ½ mile from the departure end of the runway and within 300 feet of traffic pattern altitude.

6. The primary responsibility of local tower controllers is to

    a) provide services to aircraft operating on the runways.
    b) provide radar traffic advisories to aircraft operating in the airspace around the airport.
    c) ensure that all regulations are complied with by pilots operating within their control zone.

7. In an airport area in which the control tower is equipped with tower radar displays, the _____ should still assume full responsibility for detecting possible collision hazards and avoiding them.

8. For normal approaches, the turn from base to final should be made at least how far from the approach end of the runway?

    a) ¼ mile.
    b) ½ mile.
    c) 1 mile.

9. When departing on a 45° from the airport, when should the turn to the 45° departure heading begin?

    a) When safe to do so.
    b) After reaching the 500 feet AGL.
    c) After reaching pattern altitude.

AIM §4-3-3 – Traffic Patterns

10. At some airports, the traffic patterns for propeller-driven aircraft can be as high as _____ above the ground, and with larger turbojet aircraft pattern altitudes as high as _____.

11. Enroute aircraft crossing over an airport are advised to stay

    a) well below traffic pattern altitude to avoid colliding with other air traffic.
    b) off the radio frequency to allow pilots in the traffic pattern to better coordinate.
    c) well above the traffic pattern altitude for both smaller and larger aircraft.

AIM §4-3-5 – Unexpected Maneuvers in the Airport Traffic Pattern

12. Unlike cars, airplanes cannot come to a stop for other traffic. The proper spacing of arriving aircraft using the runway can only be achieved by

    a) pilots flying in expected ways and controllers adjusting the flights as required.
    b) pilots visually determining their landing sequence based on straight-line distance from the approach end of the runway.
    c) tower controllers issuing heading vectors and airspeeds to each airplane in the pattern.

13. If needed to maintain spacing with the aircraft ahead on final, a pilot is allowed to use (without requiring explicit clearance form the tower controller)

   a) 360° turns.
   b) steep bank turns (greater than 45° bank) and sudden, extreme airspeed changes.
   c) shallow "S" turns.

14. A 360° turn should never be executed in the traffic pattern, unless

   a) requested by the controller or in emergency situations.
   b) the aircraft is #1 cleared to land.
   c) the pilot is confident that there are no aircraft in the traffic pattern operating under IFR.

AIM §4-3-6 – Use of Runways/Declared Distances

15. How would a runway be identified if its magnetic azimuth is 068°?

   a) Runway 6.
   b) Runway 68.
   c) Runway 7.

16. Which of the following would NOT be a reason for the tower controller to assign a specific runway to an arriving aircraft?

   a) The runway most nearly aligned with the current wind direction.
   b) The pre-defined "calm wind" runway, if the wind is less than 5 knots.
   c) The runway number that most closely matches the aircraft's tail number.

17. The runway distance declared and published in the Airport/Facility Directory for an airport includes the total length of all paved surface aligned with the runway direction regardless of its availability for takeoff or landing.

   a) True.
   b) False.

AIM §4-3-12 – Low approach

18. Unless otherwise authorized by ATC, a low approach, or low pass, should be made

   a) whenever the observed weather is below VFR weather minimums for the airport.
   b) with an immediate climbing right or left turn until regaining pattern altitude.
   c) straight ahead, with no turns or climb made until the pilot has made a thorough visual check for other aircraft in the area.

AIM §4-3-14 – Communications

19. When should pilots of departing aircraft contact ground control for taxi instructions?

   a) After completing engine runup.
   b) Prior to starting engines, (or just prior to taxiing if the pilot can reasonably expect no significant delay).
   c) Once they reach the runway or warm-up block.

20. Why are taxi clearances, IFR departure clearances, and other necessary communication between the tower and aircraft or utility vehicles operating on the airport delivered on a separate ground control frequency?

    a) To eliminate frequency congestion and to provide a clear VHF channel for the tower to coordinate runway use with arriving and departing aircraft.
    b) To allow pilots to be able to test their radios on two different frequencies prior to takeoff.
    c) To simplify radio communications, because the ground control frequency at all towered airports is 121.700 mHz.

21. When should a pilot that has just landed switch frequency from tower to ground?

    a) Once the wheels have touched the runway.
    b) Once the airplane has begun the turn to an exiting taxiway.
    c) When instructed to do so by the tower controller.

22. The tower controller at an airport whose Ground Control frequency is 121.600 mHz issues the instruction "Contact Ground point six". What does that mean?

    a) The pilot is required to wait at least 6 seconds before switching frequencies.
    b) The tower controller has reason to believe the pilot is familiar with the ground control frequency used at the airport and is being brief.
    c) The tower controller has authorized the pilot to change the fractional portion of the radio frequency only.

AIM §4-3-18 – Taxiing

23. Which of the following communications would be an appropriate request for taxi instructions?

    a) "Ground control, Cessna 123CW, request taxi to Runway 30."
    b) "Ground control, Cessna 123CW, at parking row Bravo, request taxi to Runway 30."
    c) "Ground control, Cessna 123CW, request taxi to Runway 30 for immediate departure."

24. Where can a pilot find the official correct way for explaining the aircraft's location on the airport to the ground controller?

    a) Airport/Facility Directory.
    b) Pilot/Controller Glossary.
    c) There is no one correct way. The pilot can choose whatever way he or she believes will appropriately convey the aircraft's location to the ground controller.

25. When an airport traffic control tower is in operation, what must the pilot have received prior to taking off, landing, or taxiing onto a runway?

    a) The correct ATIS information code.
    b) A private pilot license.
    c) An ATC clearance.

26. Which of the following would be an appropriate ground controller taxi instruction given to a waiting pilot?

    a) "Cessna 123CW, you are cleared to taxi to Runway 30 via taxiway Hotel."
    b) "Cessna 123CW, Runway 30, taxi via Hotel."
    c) "Cessna 123CW, cleared to taxi to Runway 30 via terminal."

27. When taxiing at large airports with multiple runways and taxiways, what is true of ground controller taxi instructions regarding the crossing of runways?

    a) The absence of holding instructions in a "Taxi to" clearance authorizes the pilot to cross all runways which the taxi route intersects except the assigned takeoff runway.
    b) An ATC clearance is only required when crossing an active runway.
    c) A clearance must be obtained prior to crossing any runway. ATC will use an explicit clearance for all runway crossings.

28. When ground control has issued the instruction "Cessna 123CW, taxi to and hold short of Runway 12", which of the following would be an acceptable response from the pilot?

    a) "Cessna 123CW, roger."
    b) "Cessna 123CW, Runway 12."
    c) "Cessna 123CW, hold short of Runway 12."

29. On departure, when are single-pilot aircraft with the ability to monitor multiple simultaneous radio frequencies, encouraged to begin monitoring any frequency other than the assigned ATC tower frequency?

    a) After leaving the surface area of the Class B, Class C, or Class D airspace surrounding an airport.
    b) As soon as the aircraft reaches a minimum safe altitude on departure.
    c) When instructed to do so by ATC.

30. What are progressive taxi instructions?

    a) Advanced instructions to step the aircraft up into a higher category.
    b) Step-by-step routing instructions for pilots unfamiliar with the airport.
    c) When the pilot advises the airport office that passengers will require a taxi after disembarking.

AIM §4-3-20 – Exiting the runway after landing

31. How should the pilot of an arriving aircraft exit the runway?

    a) Without delay at the first available taxiway.
    b) After coming safely to a stop, the pilot should request clearance to exit the runway.
    c) The pilot should slow (although not come to a complete stop) and wait for the tower controller to assign an exit taxiway.

32. When can a pilot come to a complete stop on a runway?

    a) Never.
    b) After first obtaining ATC approval.
    c) When the pilot needs to reverse course on the runway to reach a preferred exit taxiway.

AIM §4-3-22 – Option approach

33. When should a VFR pilot make the request for an Option Approach?

    a) Entering downwind in the traffic pattern.
    b) On final approach.
    c) Prior to entering the tower-controlled airspace.

34. When cleared for the option, a pilot is allowed to do which of the following? (Check all that apply.)

☐ Full stop landing
☐ Touch and go
☐ Land and taxi back on the runway
☐ Low approach (or low pass)
☐ Stop and go (where allowed by local airport rules)
☐ Short approach

AIM §4-3-23 – Use of aircraft lights

35. When should aircraft position lights be on?

a) When taking off after sunset.
b) Anytime the aircraft is operated on the surface or in flight from sunset to sunrise.
c) Anytime the engine is running.

36. When should the anti-collision lights be on?

a) Anytime the aircraft is in operation, except when the pilot in command determines that they would constitute a hazard to safety.
b) After the aircraft is cleared for takeoff.
c) In flight, for all operations below 10,000 feet MSL.

37. When taxiing across a runway, all external aircraft illumination should be

a) off, to minimize the blinding hazard to other pilots.
b) off, to avoid confusion with aircraft cleared for departure.
c) on, to increase the conspicuity of the aircraft to controllers and other pilots approaching to land on the runway.

38. Why are pilots encouraged to keep the landing light on when operating below 10,000 feet MSL within 10 miles of any airport?

a) Having the landing light on reduces load on the alternator.
b) To keep the light warm and prevent the accumulation of rime ice.
c) To enhance aircraft visibility, as part of the FAA's Operation Lights On safety program.

AIM §4-4-1 – ATC clearance

39. An ATC clearance is

a) authorization to proceed under specified conditions within controlled airspace.
b) a directive from ATC that overrides the pilot's responsibility of 14 CFR §91.3(a).
c) permission to deviate from any federal aviation rule or regulation.

40. If ATC issues a clearance that would place the aircraft in jeopardy, the pilot should

a) inform ATC immediately and request an amended clearance.
b) alter course or altitude to one that would be more safe.
c) submit a report to the FAA regarding the incident.

41. In which of the following situations would a pilot be expected to inform ATC of their request? (Check all that apply.)

   ☐ Preference to land on a different runway than that assigned
   ☐ Intent to perform a no-flap landing
   ☐ Disabling of the autopilot on approach
   ☐ 360° turn for spacing after established in a landing or approach sequence
   ☐ Different takeoff point preference (i.e., threshold takeoff, intersection takeoff)

AIM §4-4-13 – Runway separation

42. If the control tower issues "Cleared for immediate takeoff," what should the pilot of a departing aircraft do if he or she needs a few moments to complete the required pre-takeoff checks?

   a) Skip the checklist, but remember which items must be completed once the airplane reaches a safe altitude.
   b) Slowly start moving toward the runway while completing the remaining checks.
   c) Advise ATC that he or she is "unable" to accept immediate takeoff.

AIM §4-4-14 – Visual separation

43. If instructed by ATC to maintain visual separation from another aircraft, the pilot must

   a) turn to a heading that will take the aircraft directly away from the other traffic.
   b) keep the other aircraft completely separate from the field of view through the forward windows.
   c) maintain constant visual surveillance of the other aircraft and maneuver as required to avoid it, until it is no longer a factor.

44. If a pilot has been told to follow another aircraft, or to provide visual separation, and visual contact of the other aircraft is lost, what should the pilot do?

   a) Notify air traffic control.
   b) Execute shallow "S" turns until the other target is reacquired.
   c) Maintain current heading and altitude and increase vigilance.

Answers to Study Questions

1. b
2. c
3. a
4. b
5. c
6. a
7. pilot
8. a
9. c
10. 1,500 feet
    2,500 feet AGL
11. c
12. a
13. c
14. a
15. c
16. c
17. b (false)
18. c
19. b
20. a
21. c
22. b
23. b
24. c
25. c
26. b
27. c
28. c
29. a

30. b
31. a
32. b
33. a
34. ☒ Full stop landing
    ☒ Touch and go
    ☐ Land and taxi back on the runway
    ☒ Low approach (or low pass)
    ☒ Stop and go (where allowed by local
       airport rules)
    ☐ Short approach
35. b
36. a
37. c
38. c
39. a
40. a
41. ☒ Preference to land on a different runway
       than that assigned
    ☐ Intent to perform a no-flap landing
    ☐ Disabling of the autopilot on approach
    ☒ 360° turn for spacing after established in a
       landing or approach sequence
    ☒ Different takeoff point preference (i.e.,
       threshold takeoff, intersection takeoff)
42. c
43. c
44. a

Approaches and Landings

FTW-8A

READING ASSIGNMENT
AFH Pages 8-1 to 8-13 – "Normal Approach and Landing" through "Ground Effect"
PTS IV.B – Normal and Crosswind Approach and Landing
PTS IV.L – Go-Around/Rejected Landing

Study Questions

AFH Pages 8-1 to 8-13 – "Normal Approach and Landing" through "Ground Effect"

1. The list below includes the five phases of a normal approach and landing, but not in the correct order. Transcribe the list to the column on the right, but put the phases in the correct order.

    Roundout (flare)   1._____

    Final approach   2._____

    Ground roll   3._____

    Touchdown   4._____

    Base leg   5._____ _

2. How would a pilot factor the strength of the headwind on landing into the decision of where to fly the base leg?

    a) The pilot should fly a consistent pattern with the base leg located in the same place regardless of wind.
    b) When expecting a strong wind on final approach, the pilot should shorten the downwind and turn base closer to the runway.
    c) When expecting a strong wind on final approach, the pilot would extend the downwind and turn base farther from the runway.

3. The pilot should have the landing gear extended and a landing check completed prior to reaching the base leg.

    a) True.
    b) False.

4. How steep should the turn from base to final be?

    a) Medium.
    b) Medium to shallow.
    c) Steep.

5. At what altitude should the aircraft be at the turn from base to final?

    a) 200 feet AGL.
    b) 500 feet AGL.
    c) A safe altitude depending on the height of the terrain and any obstructions along the ground track.

6. If an extremely steep banking turn from base is needed to prevent overshooting the proper final approach path, it is advisable to

   a) retract the flaps before turning.
   b) discontinue the approach, go around, and plan to start the turn earlier on the next approach.
   c) obtain a "Steep Bank" clearance from the airport control tower before turning.

7. On final approach, how should the pilot maintain target approach speed?

   a) Extend final flaps and adjust pitch attitude as desired.
   b) Adjust throttle setting as required to keep airspeed indicator needle in the desired range.
   c) Use coordinated bank and yaw to modify drag and airspeed.

8. To control the glide angle, a pilot must use the right power setting

   a) as required for the desired airspeed, aircraft configuration (flaps, landing gear) and wind conditions.
   b) as specified in the Aeronautical Information Manual (AIM).
   c) for the given runway length.

9. Although pitch is used to control airspeed and power is used to control altitude, the pilot should remember that the two are interrelated, meaning

   a) when power is changed, the pilot must adjust control pressures to maintain the desired pitch attitude, and vice versa.
   b) that the pilot should treat the throttle and yoke as if they were one control.
   c) power should be removed before making pitch attitude changes.

10. Flaps used during landing provide several advantages including which of the following? (Check all that apply.)

    ☐ Produce greater lift at lower landing speeds.
    ☐ Reduce drag on final approach
    ☐ Reduce the length of the landing roll

11. Typically, flap deflection of up to 15° primarily produces _____ with minimal _____ and the airplane tends to balloon. Flap deflection beyond 15° produces a large increase in _____.

12. Why is it advantageous to extend flaps incrementally on downwind, base, and final rather than all at once?

    a) Allows for smaller pitch and power adjustments.
    b) It allows the airplane to reach final approach speed sooner in the traffic pattern.
    c) To allow for an increased rate of descent.

13. The diagram below shows an airplane approaching to land at three possible approach angles. The actual approach angle will depend on a variety of factors.

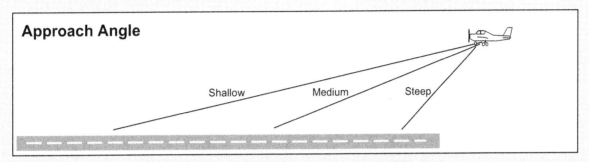

Approach Angle

Shallow   Medium   Steep

For each of the following factors, write each condition in the appropriate column that shows whether that condition will tend to result in a shallow, medium, or steep approach angle.

	Shallow	Medium	Steep
Flap Setting No flaps, Partial flaps, Full flaps	_____	_____	_____
Headwind Component Strong wind, Moderate wind, Calm	_____	_____	_____
Power Setting Idle, Low power, High power	_____	_____	_____
Approach Airspeed 55 kts, 75 kts, 95 kts	_____	_____	_____
Rudder Coordination Coordinated, Cross-controlled, Full slip	_____	_____	_____

14. On final approach, if the pilot determines the aircraft will undershoot the runway and a shallower approach is needed, the FAA recommends that

a) power and pitch should be increased.
b) flaps should be retracted.
c) full flaps should be extended (if not already)

15. Once the pilot has begun the roundout and flare, back-elevator pressure should be

a) increased as a rate that allows the airplane to continue settling slowly as forward speed decreases.
b) held constant by the pilot until all wheels are safely on the ground.
c) added in short, quick movements, coordinated with the loss of engine power.

16. In the roundout for a normal landing, power is usually

a) added slightly.
b) maintained at a constant, safe power setting.
c) reduced to idle.

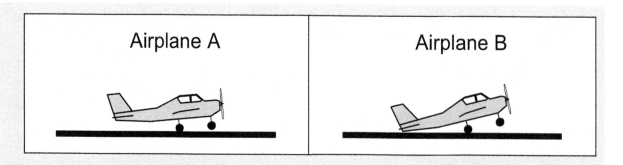

17. In the above diagram, both aircraft are touching down for a landing at the same airspeed using appropriate touch-down procedures. Using the pitch attitudes shown in the diagram as references, which airplane is landing with full flaps extended?

    a) Airplane A.
    b) Airplane B.
    c) Neither. The airplane should touchdown with all three wheels simultaneously.

18. Once roundout has started for a normal landing in a nosewheel airplane, when should the pilot push forward on the elevator control?

    a) Never.
    b) If the aircraft balloons up more than 10 feet AGL.
    c) At the moment of ground contact.

19. To prevent an excessive sink rate or a drop-in type landing, the pilot may

    a) raise the nose while simultaneously decreasing power.
    b) cut power.
    c) advance the throttle slightly.

20. The aircraft should touchdown on the main gear at approximately what airspeed?

    a) V_x.
    b) Stalling speed.
    c) 60 knots.

21. The way to make an ideal landing in a nosewheel aircraft is to

    a) fly the airplane onto the ground with excess airspeed.
    b) try to hold the airplane's wheels a few inches off the ground as long as possible.
    c) land with all three wheels touching down at the same time ("three-point landing").

22. Failure to touchdown with the airplane's longitudinal axis aligned with the runway results in

    a) a steeper descent rate.
    b) floating.
    c) severe side loads on the landing gear.

23. When is a landing considered complete?

    a) When all three wheels touch down.
    b) When the aircraft is within six inches of the ground.
    c) When the aircraft has slowed on ground roll to a normal taxi speed and the aircraft is clear of the runway.

24. Directional control (steering) in the ground roll is controlled by the

    _____

25. To increase braking capability, weight should be distributed on all three wheels equally.

    a) True.
    b) False.

26. Select the answers below that make the statements true.

    Careful application of the brakes can be initiated <u>before / after</u> the nosewheel is on the ground. Maximum braking effectiveness is just <u>short of / well before</u> the point where skidding occurs, and <u>is / is not</u> enhanced by alternately applying and reapplying brake pressure. The brakes should be applied firmly and <u>suddenly / smoothly</u> as necessary.

27. In a stabilized approach, the aircraft is moving in a steady, straight line toward the ground and the "aiming point" will appear to

    a) slide gently up the windshield.
    b) be stationary.
    c) angle up to the aircraft at a decreasing angle.

 28. What does the apparent relative movement of various ground points represent in a constant angle glidepath?

    a) Ground points that appear to move up indicate points the aircraft will overshoot.
    b) Ground points that appear stationary indicate the point at which the wheels will touch down at after a normal roundout and flare.
    c) Ground points that appear to move up indicate points the aircraft will not reach in the current glide.

29. Another visual cue for glide angle, is that the angle between the horizon and the aiming point should be

    _____.

 30. If the trapezoidal shape of the landing runway appears to be much wider at the base than at the top, the aircraft is

    a) too low.
    b) too high.
    c) possibly high or low. It cannot be determined from the given information.

31. In a stabilized approach, the airplane should be trimmed in such a way that the aiming point can be reached

    a) with hands off.
    b) with only small S-turns.
    c) regardless of adjustments to flap settings.

32. Common errors in approach and landing include:

    • Un_____ approach.
    • Overshooting the turn onto final approach resulting in _____ a turn.
    • Failure to adequately compensate for _____ extension.
    • Attempting to maintain an altitude or reach the runway using _____ alone.
    • Touchdown prior to attaining the proper _____.
    • Failure to hold sufficient _____-elevator pressure after touchdown.

Slips

33. Intentional slips can be used to

    a) reduce drag on landing.
    b) dissipate altitude without increasing airspeed.
    c) achieve increased fuel efficiency.

34. A slip is a combination of what two types of movement?

    a) Rolling and spinning.
    b) Forward and sideward.
    c) Upward and outward.

★ 35. In a forward slip, the rudder is used to pull the nose of the airplane to the side and the wings are

    a) banked in the opposite direction.
    b) held level with the natural horizon.
    c) rocked back and forth to create dynamic drag.

36. The steepness of a slip in most light airplanes is limited by

    a) the amount of rudder travel available.
    b) a roll limit in the yoke.
    c) regulation.

37. To discontinue a slip, release the _____ pressure and _____ the wings while readjusting the _____ to normal glide attitude.

38. In a forward slip, the nose points _____; in a sideslip the nose points _____.

Go Arounds

39. Which of the following are reasons to go around? (Check all that apply.)

   ☐ Hazard on the runway
   ☐ ATC instructions
   ☐ Wind shear
   ☐ Unstabilized approach
   ☐ Wake turbulence
   ☐ Runway free of other aircraft
   ☐ Unsatisfactory landing conditions

40. The go around should be used

   a) in emergency situations only.
   b) only when instructed to do so.
   c) as an alternative to any approach and/or landing.

41. When executing a go around, the pilot's attention should move swiftly to make the appropriate changes in

   a) altitude, power, and attitude.
   b) power, attitude, and configuration.
   c) bank, roll, and yaw.

42. When is a go around dangerous?

   a) Always.
   b) When executed improperly or when the decision to go around has been made late.
   c) When flaps are extended.

43. A go around should be performed at

   a) full power or maximum takeoff power.
   b) 75% power.
   c) a power setting appropriate for maintaining the airplane's altitude.

44. How can maximum power be assured in an aircraft equipped with a carburetor?

   a) Smooth, positive throttle application, with carburetor heat turned off.
   b) Abrupt, responsive full throttle with carburetor hear applied.
   c) Power should be brought only to 75% to allow the carburetor fuel reservoir to adequately refill.

45. In a go around, the pitch attitude must be managed in such a way as to allow for sufficient buildup of

   _____ before any effort is made to gain _____.

46. In a go around, the pilot should retract the flaps

   a) from full to partial to reduce drag and allow the aircraft to gain airspeed for the climb.
   b) after reaching traffic pattern altitude.
   c) first, then add power to climb.

47. An airplane that has been properly trimmed for approach will tend to _____ when full power is applied in a go around, unless the pilot maintains positive control.

    a) drop the nose.
    b) raise the nose suddenly.
    c) strongly pull to the right.

48. Common errors in the performance of go arounds include:

    a) In_____.
    b) _____ in initiating a go around.
    c) Abrupt _____ application.
    d) Improper pitch _____.
    e) Failure to compensate for _____/_____.

PTS IV.B – Normal and Crosswind Approach and Landing

49. What factors should a pilot take into consideration when selecting a suitable touchdown point?

    a) Runway heading, intensity of ground lighting, and landing surface.
    b) Wind conditions, number of taxiways, and location of rotating beacon.
    c) Landing surface, wind conditions, and obstructions.

50. What type of approach will best demonstrate a pilot's mastery of pitch and power required for landing?

    a) High-speed approach.
    b) Dog-leg base to final.
    c) Stabilized approach.

51. If V_{S0} for your airplane is 40 knots and the POH recommended approach speed is 65 knots, what airspeed would meet FAA Practical Test Standards?

    a) 40 knots.
    b) 52 knots.
    c) 65 knots.

52. At what speed should the pilot demonstrate touching the aircraft down on the runway?

    a) Approach speed +10/-5 knots.
    b) Approximate stalling speed.
    c) V_A.

PTS IV.L – Go-Around/Rejected Landing

53. In performing a go around, what is just as important as using the correct technique?

    a) Maintaining a consistent airspeed throughout.
    b) Making the decision to go around in a timely, fashion, using good judgment.
    c) Retracting the flaps immediately.

54. The instant the decision has been made to go around, the pilot should

    a) apply full or takeoff power immediately to build airspeed and transition to a climb pitch attitude.
    b) retract the flaps and lower the nose to pickup airspeed.
    c) slide to the left of the runway centerline.

55. How long should takeoff power and V_Y airspeed be maintained?

    a) Until at least 100 feet above the surface of the runway.
    b) Until reaching traffic pattern altitude.
    c) Until reaching a safe maneuvering altitude.

 56. What does it mean to retract flaps "as appropriate"?

    a) After reaching V_Y with a positive rate of climb.
    b) Once the airplane begins to climb.
    c) After reaching a speed of V_Y or greater.

Answers to Study Questions

1. 1. Base leg
    2. Final approach
    3. Roundout (flare)
    4. Touchdown
    5. Ground roll

2. b

3. a (true)

4. b

5. c

6. b

7. a

8. a

9. a

10. ☒ Produce greater lift at lower landing speeds
    ☐ Reduce drag on final approach
    ☒ Reduce the length of the landing roll)

11. lift
    drag
    drag

12. a

13.
No flaps	Partial flaps	Full flaps
Calm	Moderate wind	Strong wind
High power	Low power	Idle
95 kts	75 kts	55 kts
Coordinated	Cross-controlled	Full slip

14. a

15. a

16. c

17. a

18. a

19. c

20. b

21. b

22. c

23. c

24. rudder, steerable nosewheel (if present), and toe brakes

25. b (false)

26. after
    just short of
    is not
    smoothly

27. b

28. c

29. constant

30. a

31. a

32. stabilized
    too steep
    flap
    pitch
    landing attitude
    back

33. b

34. b

35. a

36. a

37. rudder
    level
    pitch attitude

38. to the side
    forward

39. ☒ Hazard on the runway
    ☒ ATC instructions
    ☒ Wind shear
    ☒ Unstabilized approach
    ☒ Wake turbulence
    ☐ Runway free of other aircraft
    ☒ Unsatisfactory landing conditions

40. c

41. b

42. b

43. a

44. a

45. airspeed
    altitude

46. a

47. b

48. decision
    Delay
    power
    attitude
    torque/P-factor

49. c

50. c

51. c

52. b

53. b

54. a

55. c

56. a

Crosswind Approach and Landing

READING ASSIGNMENT

AFH Pages 8-13 to 8-17 – "Crosswind Approach and Landing" through "Turbulent Air Approach and Landing"

Study Questions

1. The two methods for accomplishing a crosswind approach and landing are the

   _____ method and the _____ method.

2. In the wing-low method, the pilot aligns the airplanes heading with

   a) the direction of the relative wind.
   b) the centerline of the runway.
   c) magnetic north.

3. When the initial wind drift is observed, the pilot should promptly correct for the drift by

   a) lowering the wing on the side the wind is coming from.
   b) lowering the downwind wing.
   c) holding the wings level, while adjusting rudder to cancel the drift.

4. How does the roundout and flare differ for a crosswind landing as compared to a normal landing?

   a) They are the same.
   b) Crosswind roundouts should be more sudden.
   c) One wing will be low throughout.

5. In a properly executed crosswind landing the touchdown will occur on

   a) the nosewheel.
   b) both main landing gear.
   c) the upwind main wheel.

 6. What does the pilot use the rudder pedals for during the touchdown portion of a crosswind landing?

   a) To keep the nose aligned with the runway centerline.
   b) To balance the aircraft on one wheel.
   c) To correct for crosswind drift.

7. What does the pilot use the ailerons for during the touchdown portion of a crosswind landing?

   a) To maintain directional control.
   b) To maintain the bank angle that cancels the lateral drift.
   c) To increase drag and reduce the groundspeed.

8. With the main landing gear acting as a pivot point and a greater surface area exposed to the wind behind the pivot point, the airplane will tend to

   _____

9. Contacting the runway with a side load from improper drift correction or runway alignment could result in

   a) a longer ground roll.
   b) damage to the landing gear or the aircraft tipping over.
   c) stronger ground effect and ballooning.

10. The increased drag during a sideslip used in a crosswind landing can result in

   a) excessive sink rate and/or too low an airspeed.
   b) prolonged flare and longer ground roll.
   c) a spinning stall.

11. A clear indication of pilot error in the performance of a crosswind landing is

   a) touchdown on one wheel.
   b) touchdown while drifting.
   c) active use of rudder.

12. Gusty wind conditions may require the use of

   a) partial (less than full) wing flaps and an increased approach airspeed.
   b) full flaps and a steeper descent angle.
   c) no flaps and a slower approach speed.

13. If the normal approach speed is 70 knots and the current wind is at 8 knots with gusts up to 14 knots, what would be the new approach airspeed a pilot would use for the wind conditions?

   a) 60 knots.
   b) 73 knots.
   c) 78 knots.

14. Touchdown in turbulent conditions should be at a

   a) level flight attitude with only enough nose up pitch to prevent the nosewheel from contacting the ground before the main landing gear.
   b) Nose high pitch attitude with minimal aileron use.
   c) Nose high pitch attitude with immediate, positive use of the ailerons.

Answers to Study Questions

1. crab; wing-low (sideslip)
2. b
3. a
4. c
5. c
6. a
7. b

8. weathervane into the wind
9. b
10. a
11. b
12. a
13. b
14. a

Short-Field Approach and Landing

READING ASSIGNMENT
AFH Pages 8-17 to 8-19 – "Short-Field Approach and Landing"
PTS IV.F – Short-Field Approach and Landing

Study Questions

AFH Pages 8-17 to 8-19 – "Short-Field Approach and Landing"

1. Which two of the following approach and landing situations merit the use of short-field techniques?

   ☐ Uneven or soft runway landing surface
   ☐ Approach path made over obstacles that limit the available landing area
   ☐ Landing with suspected landing gear failure
   ☐ Landing at fields with relatively short runways

2. Properly executing a short-field approach and landing demands a high degree of pilot competency, as

   a) the airplane is flown at an airspeed approaching the minimal controllable airspeed while operating very low to the ground.
   b) the airspeeds used are dangerously close to the design maneuvering speed.
   c) the airplane is typically landed on the nose wheel first to reduce ground roll (for nosewheel-equipped airplanes).

3. An ideal short-field landing would be one in which

   a) the nosewheel does not contact the ground until the aircraft has almost come to a stop.
   b) a stable, shallower than normal approach angle is used throughout the approach.
   c) there is little or no floating during the roundout.

4. Typically, a short-field landing is made without the use of flaps to increase the angle of descent.

   a) True.
   b) False.

5. If in the POH the airplane manufacturer specifies an airspeed and flap configuration that is to be used during short-field approaches, the pilot should

   a) use those values for short-field approaches.
   b) operate at half the stated values until pilot proficiency is reached.
   c) decrease the airspeed by the size of the gust factor if any.

6. In the absence of a manufacturer-specified, short-field approach airspeed, how fast should a short-field approach be flown if the power-off stalling speed in a landing configuration is 40 knots?

    a) No faster than 48 knots.
    b) No faster than 52 knots.
    c) At or above V_Y until clear of the obstacles.

 7. If V_{s0} for your airplane is 50 knots, and the current wind is at 10 knots with gusts up to 14 knots, what would be the fastest approach airspeed a pilot would use in making a short-field approach and landing?

    a) 52 knots.
    b) 67 knots.
    c) 74 knots.

8. In practicing short-field landings at airports with long runways and approach paths free of obstacles, the pilot should treat the approach as

    a) a normal approach and landing.
    b) an accuracy approach to a spot landing.
    c) a power-off glide.

9. Excessively low airspeed can result in a dangerous rate of descent because

    a) available engine power may not be sufficient to overcome the increase in drag and may only result in a further rate of descent.
    b) excessive nose-down pitch attitude increases drag.
    c) flaps must be retracted in order to clear the final obstacles.

10. For a short-field landing, the aircraft should touch down at MCA, which is

    a) maximum clearance angle.
    b) multiple channel advisory.
    c) minimum controllable airspeed.

11. Upon touchdown, the airplane should be held in the same positive pitch attitude for as long as the elevators remain effective, to provide aerodynamic braking and assist in deceleration.

    a) True.
    b) False.

12. For maximum braking on the ground roll, many aircraft manufacturers recommend that flaps be retracted on landing. Why would this be?

    a) The movement of the flap retraction motor provides aerodynamic drag.
    b) Retracting the flaps increases the weight on the landing gear and allows for additional braking without sliding.
    c) Early flap retraction frees the pilot from one task that would have to be done at shutdown.

13. Select the answers that indicate some common errors in the performance of short-field approaches and landings.

- Too <u>low / high</u> an airspeed, resulting in floating on roundout.
- Too <u>low / high</u> an airspeed on final, resulting in inability to flare properly and landing hard.
- Failure to allow enough <u>room / airspeed</u> on final to set up the approach.
- Flying a(n) <u>stabilized / unstabilized</u> approach.
- Prematurely reducing <u>power / mixture</u> to idle on roundout, resulting in hard landing.
- Failure to maintain <u>radio / directional</u> control on the ground roll.

PTS IV.F – Short-Field Approach and Landing

14. On a FAA Practical Test ("checkride"), who selects a suitable touchdown spot for the demonstration of a short-field approach and landing?

    a) The FAA-designated pilot examiner.
    b) The applicant, acting as pilot-in-command.
    c) The tower controller.

15. If, in the POH, the airplane manufacturer specifies an airspeed to be used during short-field approaches, the pilot should maintain that airspeed

    a) ± 5 knots.
    b) ± 10 knots.
    c) +10/-5 knots.

16. When should crosswind correction be maintained during a short-field approach and landing?

    a) Until the first wheel touches the runway.
    b) Until all landing gear are firmly on the surface.
    c) Throughout the approach and landing sequence.

17. The PTS standards for short-field landings specify that the aircraft touch down at a point at or within _____ of the intended touchdown point.

    a) 50 feet.
    b) 100 feet.
    c) 200 feet.

18. Failure of the pilot to maintain the airplane's longitudinal axis in alignment with and over the runway centerline would

    a) be acceptable, provided the intended touchdown point was reached.
    b) be considered a failed demonstration of the short-field approach and landing task in the PTS.
    c) subject the pilot to FAA fines or other penalties.

Answers to Study Questions

1. ☐ Uneven or soft runway landing surface
   ☒ Approach path made over obstacles that limit the available landing area
   ☐ Landing with suspected landing gear failure
   ☒ Landing at fields with relatively short runways

2. a

3. c

4. b (false)

5. a

6. b

7. b

8. b

9. a

10. c

11. a (true)

12. b

13. high
    low
    room
    unstabilized
    power
    directional

14. b

15. c

16. c

17. c

18. b

Soft-Field Approach and Landing

READING ASSIGNMENT

AFH Pages 8-19 to 8-20 – "Soft-Field Approach and Landing"
PTS IV.D – Soft-Field Approach and Landing

Study Questions

AFH Pages 8-19 to 8-20 – "Soft-Field Approach and Landing"

1. One goal for landing on any runway should be to land at

   a) the slowest possible landing speed.
   b) the midpoint of the runway.
   c) traffic pattern altitude.

2. When landing on fields that are rough or have soft surfaces such as snow, sand, or grass, an additional goal should be to

   a) transfer the weight of the aircraft from the wings to the wheels as soon as possible.
   b) decelerate as quickly as possible.
   c) touch down as smoothly as possible.

3. There is danger associated with landing on soft or rough surface runways because

   a) of the stresses imposed on the landing gear by drag and irregular surface shape.
   b) the landings are done at very high airspeeds.
   c) the airplane will tend to float considerably farther in ground effect than normal.

 4. If the airplane sets down hard on the main landing gear, it can create a

   a) nose-over force, which could cause the nose wheel to stick into a soft surface.
   b) left-turning tendency, which could slide the aircraft off the runway.
   c) surge in airspeed, which could extend the landing roll.

5. At touchdown on a soft field, engine power is increased slightly to

   a) increase ground effect.
   b) increase airspeed.
   c) slow the descent rate and cushion the landing.

6. Which wheels touch down first in a well-executed soft-field landing in a tricycle gear airplane?

   a) Nosewheel.
   b) Main landing gear.
   c) All three wheels should touch down at the same time.

7. To minimize the hazards associated with soft or rough runways, support of the airplane's weight

   a) is controlled primarily through smooth aileron and rudder movements at touchdown.
   b) must be transferred from the wings to the wheels as smoothly as possible during the landing roll.
   c) is borne only by the main landing gear.

8. The use of brakes on a soft field is

   a) not needed and should be avoided.
   b) critical to maintaining a smooth transition from flight to the ground roll.
   c) considered preferable to rudder/nosewheel steering.

9. One common error in the performance of soft-field landings is

   a) flying a stabilized approach.
   b) allowing the nosewheel to fall to the runway after touchdown rather than controlling its descent.
   c) touching down on the main landing gear only.

PTS IV.D – Soft-Field Approach and Landing

 10. Unless otherwise specified by the manufacturer, the final approach speed recommended by the PTS for a soft-field landing is

   a) faster than that used in a short-field landing.
   b) slower than that used in a short-field landing.
   c) appropriate for use in a short-field landing, as well.

11. Which of the following are important to the successful demonstration of a soft-field approach and landing? (Check all that apply.)

   ☐ Lands over the runway centerline with no drift
   ☐ Touches down softly
   ☐ Stops within 200 feet of the intended touchdown point
   ☐ Maintains aft elevator and sufficient speed to taxi on a soft surface
   ☐ Lands with minimal flare distance

Answers to Study Questions

1. a

2. c

3. a

4. a

5. c

6. b

7. b

8. a

9. b

10. c

11. ☒ Lands over the runway centerline with no drift
☒ Touches down softly
☐ Stops within 200 feet of the intended touchdown point
☒ Maintains aft elevator and sufficient speed to taxi on a soft surface
☐ Lands with minimal flare distance

Power-Off Accuracy Approaches

READING ASSIGNMENT

AFH Pages 8-21 to 8-25 – "Power-off Accuracy Approaches" through
                        "360° Power-off Approach"

PTS IV.K – Forward Slip to a Landing

Study Questions

AFH Pages 8-21 to 8-25 – "Power-off Accuracy Approaches" through
                        "360° Power-off Approach"

1. Judgment of altitude in hundreds of feet is not as important to a pilot making a power off approach as is

    a) the ability to estimate the distance the airplane will glide to a landing.
    b) the ability to react to changes in altitude w/power.
    c) correct metering of fuel flow over time.

2. The diagram below shows three possibilities for a pilot making a 180° power-off approach to a runway. The pilot determines the appropriate place to turn onto the base leg based on a variety of factors, including winds, height, and availability of flaps.

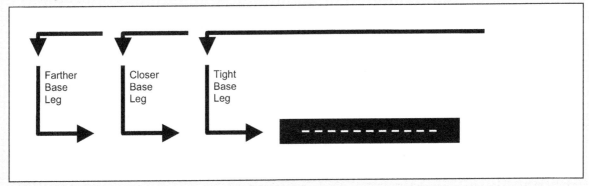

For each of the following situations, identify the appropriate location for the base leg.

	Farther Base	Closer Base	Tight Base
Normal winds on runway	☐ Farther Base	☐ Closer Base	☐ Tight Base
Very strong winds on runway	☐ Farther Base	☐ Closer Base	☐ Tight Base
Inoperative flaps	☐ Farther Base	☐ Closer Base	☐ Tight Base
Very low altitude	☐ Farther Base	☐ Closer Base	☐ Tight Base
Very high altitude	☐ Farther Base	☐ Closer Base	☐ Tight Base

3. In the diagram, Glidepath A shows the approach path for an airplane approaching to land in a power-off approach at best glide airspeed.

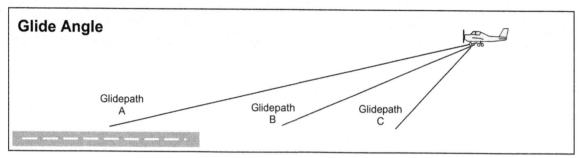

Which glidepath would likely result, if the approach airspeed used was slightly lower than best glide airspeed?

a) Glidepath A.
b) Glidepath B.
c) Glidepath C.

4. Which glidepath would result if the pilot put the airplane into a full forward slip?

a) Glidepath A.
b) Glidepath B.
c) Glidepath C.

5. Execution of a 90° power off approach should begin at

a) 500 feet AGL.
b) 1,000 feet AGL or normal traffic pattern altitude.
c) 2,000 feet AGL.

6. For a 360° power off approach, the aircraft should be at approximately 2,000 feet AGL and positioned

_____

_____

_____

7. Which of the following errors could result in the aircraft settling to the ground short of reaching the intended landing areas? (Check all that apply.)

☐ Downwind leg too wide of the runway.
☐ Overextension of downwind leg resulting from tailwind.
☐ Inadequate compensation of wind drift on base leg.
☐ Failure to lower landing gear.
☐ Premature flap extension.

PTS, IV.K, Forward Slip to a Landing

 8. When forward slipping to lose altitude, the pilot should use

    a) bank control.
    b) bank and yaw control.
    c) bank and yaw control, with pitch adjustment as appropriate.

9. In a forward slip to a landing, the runway centerline should be aligned with

    a) the longitudinal axis of the airplane.
    b) the airplane's ground track.
    c) the lateral axis on the upwind side.

 10. After completing a forward slip and returning to a normal approach, the runway centerline should now be aligned with

    a) the relative wind.
    b) the longitudinal axis.
    c) the curve of the engine cowling.

11. How should control applications be made during the slip?

    a) Aggessively, with sudden jumping movements.
    b) In a smooth, timely and correct manner.
    c) Using control pressures only with little or no discernible movement of the aircraft.

Answers to Study Questions

1. a

2.

Normal winds on runway	☐ Farther Base	☒ Closer Base	☐ Tight Base
Very strong winds on runway	☐ Farther Base	☐ Closer Base	☒ Tight Base
Inoperative flaps	☒ Farther Base	☐ Closer Base	☐ Tight Base
Very low altitude	☐ Farther Base	☐ Closer Base	☒ Tight Base
Very high altitude	☒ Farther Base	☐ Closer Base	☐ Tight Base

3. b

4. c

5. b

6. over the approach end of the landing runway, or slightly to the side of it, with the airplane headed in the proposed landing direction and the landing gear and flaps retracted

7.
   ☒ Downwind leg too wide of the runway
   ☒ Overextension of downwind leg resulting from tailwind
   ☒ Inadequate compensation of wind drift on base leg
   ☐ Failure to lower landing gear
   ☒ Premature flap extension

8. c

9. b

10. b

11. b

Emergency Approaches and Landing

READING ASSIGNMENT
Pilot's Operating Handbook, Emergency Procedures, Engine Failures
AFH Pages 8-25 to 8-27 – "Emergency Approaches and Landings (Simulated)"

Study Questions

Pilot's Operating Handbook, Emergency Procedures, Engine Failures

1. In the Emergency Procedures section of a POH, what is typically indicated by emergency procedure steps that are shown in boldface type?

   a) The steps should be memorized.
   b) The steps are optional.
   c) Additional information regarding those steps is contained in the amplified procedures section of the POH.

2. Why are the emergency procedures for dealing with an engine failure just after takeoff different from the procedures for dealing with an engine failure in flight?

   a) The best glide airspeeds are significantly different and result in very different glide angles.
   b) Engine failures at altitude may allow time for restart procedures to be attempted.
   c) If the wheels have not stopped spinning from the takeoff roll, the aerodynamics of the forced landing will be substantially different.

3. When responding to an engine failure immediately after takeoff, or for any forced landing, why is it a good idea to shutdown and secure the engine prior to landing?

   a) Having the engine on limits the effectiveness of flaps and ailerons.
   b) To reduce the possibility of a post-crash fire.
   c) To reserve some fuel for future takeoffs, if needed.

4. When should the airplane's avionics and electrical system be shut down during a forced landing?

   a) Once landing is assured.
   b) Prior to squawking 7700 on the transponder.
   c) After the aircraft comes to a complete stop.

AFH Pages 8-25 to 8-27 – "Emergency Approaches and Landings (Simulated)"

5. What should the pilot immediately do when the flight instructor announces "simulated engine failure" or "simulated emergency landing"?

   a) Quickly review the positions and indications of the engine controls to see if the engine can be restarted.
   b) Review the available emergency landing areas and narrow the list of potential landing spots to 3 or 4.
   c) Establish the proper glide attitude and configuration and trim to maintain that speed.

6. The goal during the glide portion of an emergency landing should be

   a) to arrive at the normal key position at a normal traffic pattern altitude for the selected landing area.
   b) to minimize turns and increase gliding range.
   c) to determine wind direction from smoke, dust, and windmills.

7. What are the hazards associated with changing the pilot's initial selection of emergency landing area?

   a) Operations at low altitudes violate many communities' noise abatement laws.
   b) Excessive maneuvering leads to rapid altitude decay and at low altitudes this can be extremely dangerous.
   c) The delay in transit time increases the likelihood of carburetor icing.

8. One of the most common errors of inexperienced pilots during simulated emergency landings is to arrive at the edge of the landing area with too much _____ to permit a safe landing.

9. Which of the following are recommended ways to adjust glide angle and arrive at the correct aiming spot during a simulated emergency landing? (Check all that apply.)

   ☐ Increasing engine RPM
   ☐ Varying the position of the base leg
   ☐ Slipping the airplane
   ☐ Varying the turn onto final approach
   ☐ Using flaps

10. Why would a flight instructor keep his or her hand on the throttle throughout the simulated engine failure?

    a) To calm the fears of student pilots.
    b) To periodically warm and clear the engine, and take complete control of the throttle.
    c) To keep changes in atmospheric pressure from moving the throttle control.

11. When should a simulated emergency landing approach be terminated?

    a) When it can be determined whether a safe landing could have been made.
    b) When the main wheels have safely touched down on the emergency landing area.
    c) At or above 1,500 feet AGL.

Engine Failure Procedures

1. Best Glide

   • Establish and maintain the recommended best-glide airspeed

2. Landing area

   • Select a suitable landing area
   • Turn toward landing area

As Time Permits

3. Systems Flow Check

   • Check fuel system controls, air intake, spark

4. Airplane Emergency Checklist

   • Follow the appropriate checklist

5. Call for Help

   • 121.5 emergency frequency, or a nearby ATC frequency
   • 7700 transponder
   • ELT

---

6. Approach

   • Plan and follow a flight path to the key position of the selected landing area considering altitude, wind, terrain, and obstructions

---

As Time Permits

7. Secure aircraft for forced landing

   • Shut off engine and fuel flow
   • Shut off electrical system when no longer needed
   • Use padding to shield occupants

---

8. Forced landing

   • Seatbelts fastened
   • Doors unlatched
   • Land at slowest possible touchdown speed
   • Fly the aircraft until it stops, shielding the fuselage and occupants as much as possible

FTW-8F

12. Why is establishing the best glide airspeed the first and most important step in a simulated engine failure?

   a) FAA flight examiners can clearly see the airspeed indicator during flight and tend to put unnecessary emphasis on airspeed maintenance.
   b) To immediately establish the right nose-up attitude for a forced landing.
   c) Establishing best glide airspeed gives the pilot more time to respond to the emergency and a greater glide distance in which to select a safe landing area.

13. Is there any advantage to the pilot to trim the aircraft once best glide airspeed has been established?

   a) No, if the speed is maintained it makes no difference if the aircraft is trimmed for hands-free operation.
   b) No, because the elevator trim system is inoperative in the event of an engine failure.
   c) Yes, because it frees more of the pilot's attention for other important tasks.

14. Any delay in turning toward a suitable landing area is doubly damaging, because the airplane loses

   _____ while flying the wrong direction before turning, and lose more while retracing the path back to the selected landing site.

15. In responding to an emergency engine failure on takeoff or at very low altitude, when there is little or no time before ground contact is made, which of the following actions should still be done? (Check all that apply.)

   ☐ Establish best glide speed
   ☐ Select and aim for a suitable landing area
   ☐ Complete the emergency checklist from the aircraft POH
   ☐ Set your transponder
   ☐ Attempt to restart the engine at least three times before calling for help
   ☐ Complete a forced landing to the best of your ability

16. Stresses on the landing gear and other impact forces on the fuselage can be minimized if the aircraft is landed at

   a) a normal approach speed.
   b) the lowest possible touchdown speed.
   c) an airspeed at or above V_A.

17. The reason for seatbelts is obvious, but what is the best reason for unlatching and opening the doors prior to landing?

   a) To allow more air into the cockpit to calm the pilot.
   b) To prevent the doors from jamming shut in a hard landing and making exit difficult.
   c) To increase parasite drag and slow down the aircraft.

18. What transponder code can be used to alert air traffic control to the fact that you are in an emergency situation?

   a) 1200.
   b) 911.
   c) 7700.

19. If time permits, why might the pilot complete a systems flow check and review all engine and system controls BEFORE calling for help?

    a) To improve the response time from Air Traffic Control.
    b) To gain more information about the emergency that can be relayed to ATC.
    c) To avoid declaring an unnecessary emergency, if the engine can be restarted following simple corrections to the controls (e.g., fuel on different tank, mixture rich, magnetos set to both).
    d) Both b and c.

20. Select the answers below that make the statements true.

    In responding to an altitude increase / engine failure , if time permits, the pilot should complete a systems flow check followed immediately / after landing by the completion of the airplane's engine failure checklist in the POH / FARs . The systems flow check is usually completed from memory, and the flow pattern covers the entire instrument panel and console mounted pitch trim / engine controls . One such flow check is often referred to as a "seven up" flow check, because the pilot's / controller's eyes scan from the center bottom of the console and upward and across the panel switches from right to left tracing an upward "7" shape, checking along the way that all controls and switches are as required / in the off position .

    The airplane manufacturer's recommended engine failure checklist / placard should also be completed to ensure that all controls and switches / lights and radios are in their proper positions for normal engine operation. Often, the manufacturer will include an air restart procedure to attempt to shutdown / restart the engine while still in the air. The engine failure checklist should be completed by reference to the aircraft POH or other checklist / airworthiness certificate .

21. If an engine failure occurs while flying not in the vicinity of an airport control tower or while not in contact with approach control or an air route traffic control center, emergency assistance should be available on what frequency?

    _____

22. After selecting a suitable emergency landing area, what other factors should the pilot include in deciding what flight path to follow to the landing area?

    a) The condition of the landing gear and the amount of remaining tread available on the wheels.
    b) Altitude, wind, terrain and obstructions.
    c) Pressure, humidity, and outside air temperature.

23. When a forced landing is unavoidable, the pilot should operate the flight and engine controls and "fly the aircraft" until

    a) told to abandon the approach by air traffic control.
    b) initial ground contact.
    c) the aircraft has stopped moving and the engine has been shut down.

Answers to Study Questions

1. a
2. b
3. b
4. a
5. c
6. a
7. b
8. speed
9. ☐ Increasing engine RPM
   ☒ Varying the position of the base leg
   ☒ Slipping the airplane
   ☒ Varying the turn onto final approach
   ☒ Using flaps
10. b
11. a
12. c
13. c
14. altitude
15. ☒ Establish best glide speed
    ☒ Select and turn to a suitable landing area
    ☐ Complete the emergency checklist from the aircraft POH
    ☐ Set your transponder
    ☐ Shut off the engine and electrical system
    ☒ Complete a forced landing to the best of your ability

16. b
17. b
18. c
19. d
20. engine failure
    immediately
    POH
    engine controls
    pilot's
    as required
    checklist
    controls and switches
    restart
    other checklist
21. 121.500 mHz
22. b
23. c

Faulty Approaches and Landings

READING ASSIGNMENT
AFH Pages 8-27 to 8-35 – "Faulty Approaches and Landings"

Study Questions

 1. Which of the following would be sufficient cause to abort the approach and go around?

a) Slightly low final approach airspeed.
b) Moderately high final approach airspeed.
c) Excessively low or excessively high final approach airspeed.

2. On landing and touchdown, if too slow and too low, it is best to _____.

3. If during the landing flare the roundout is made too rapidly, the plane's descent stops or the plane rises slightly, the pilot should correct for this by

a) lowering the nose.
b) pitching up further to slow the aircraft.
c) holding the pitch attitude constant until the airplane decelerates enough to again start descending.

4. If the roundout has been made so high and it appears the nose must be lowered significantly to reach the runway, the pilot should

a) lower the nose only enough to begin a normal descent rate.
b) initiate a go around.
c) reduce power and lower the nose to increase airspeed.

5. If the roundout is late, the nosewheel

a) may strike the runway first, in which case the pilot should go around.
b) should be held on the runway until the main landing gear have made contact.
c) should be held very high until speed decreases.

6. What causes floating during roundout?

a) Excessive flaps.
b) Sideslipping.
c) Too much airspeed on final approach.

7. If the aircraft balloons slightly in the flare, and there is sufficient runway available, the pilot should

    a) maintain a constant landing attitude and consider using power as airspeed decreases to cushion the landing.
    b) go around.
    c) cut power and lower the nose to the runway.

8. If airspeed is too fast and the pilot attempts to force the airplane onto the ground when it still wants to fly, what can result?

    a) Porpoising.
    b) Low altitude stall.
    c) Hydroplaning.

9. Define the following terms:

    wheelbarrowing _____

    ground loop _____

    hydroplaning _____

Answers to Study Questions

1. c
2. execute a go around.
3. c
4. b
5. a
6. c
7. a

8. a
9. When weight or pressure is concentrated on the nosewheel, with the airplane's momentum pushing from behind

    An uncontrolled turn during ground operation, especially during the ground roll

    When water, slush, or wet snow causes a sudden loss of braking ability, as the wheels ride on a cushion or water

FTW-8G

Steep Turns

READING ASSIGNMENT
AFH Pages 9-1 to 9-2 – "Steep Turns"
PTS V – Steep Turns

Study Questions

AFH Pages 9-1 to 9-2 – "Steep Turns"

1. A steep turn maneuver consists of a turn in either direction using a bank angle between

    a) 10° to 30°.
    b) 45° to 60°.
    c) 90° to 120°.

2. The additional load factor in a steep turn has the effect of raising the

    a) stall speed.
    b) weight.
    c) dihedral.

3. The diagrams below show the angles of attack used by two identical airplanes flown in straight and level flight at 70 knots. The only difference between the two airplanes is that one has more weight carried onboard the aircraft.

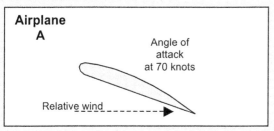 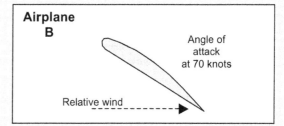

If the airplanes are identical and the angles of attack required to hold altitude are as shown, which airplane is carrying the greater weight?

a) Airplane A.
b) Airplane B.
c) It cannot be determined from the airspeeds and angles of attack shown.

★ 4. The diagram on the left below shows the angle of attack required by an airplane when flying in straight and level flight.

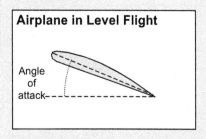 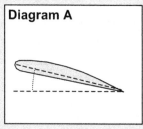 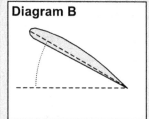

Airplane in Level Flight

Angle of attack

Diagram A

Diagram B

Which of the diagrams on the right shows the angles of attack required by the same airplane to maintain altitude while flying in a steep turn?

a) Diagram A.
b) Diagram B.
c) It cannot be determined from the airspeeds and angles of attack shown.

5. How does the critical angle of attack (the angle of attack at which the airfoil will stall) change for an airplane flying in a steep turn?

a) The critical angle of attack increases.
b) The critical angle of attack decreases.
c) The critical angle of attack does not change.

6. How does the stall speed change for an airplane flying in a steep turn?

a) The stall speed increases.
b) The stall speed decreases.
c) The stall speed does not change.

7. As an airplane is being established in a steep turn _____ pressure should be smoothly increased to increase the angle of attack (and provide greater lift).

8. Why is power added in the performance of a steep turn?

a) To overcome increased drag and maintain the entry altitude and airspeed.
b) To reduce the load factor and decrease drag.
c) To decrease the turn radius.

9. In a steep turn, the pilot's eyes should

a) be focused on the aircraft's nose.
b) move between the nose, the horizon, and the wings.
c) jump between the wingtips and the attitude indicator.

10. What control adjustments might the pilot make while attempting to hold altitude in a steep turn? (Check all that apply.)

☐ Bank angle changes of 1° to 3°.
☐ Increasing or relaxing back elevator pressure.
☐ Coordinated use of aileron and rudder.

11. When rolling out from a steep turn,

    a) back elevator pressure is reduced and the nose is raised.
    b) back elevator pressure is increased and the nose is raised.
    c) back elevator pressure is reduced and the nose is lowered.

12. Fill in the blanks to show common errors in the performance of steep turns.

    • Failure to adequately _____.
    • Inadequate _____ management and/or _____ control.
    • Attempting to perform the maneuver by _____ rather than by visual _____.
    • Failure to scan for _____ during the maneuver.
    • Excessive pitch change during _____ or _____.

PTS V – Steep Turns

13. At what speed should the steep turn be performed?

    a) 100 knots.
    b) V_{NO}.
    c) The manufacturer's recommended airspeed, if stated.

14. What range of bank angles would acceptably demonstrate mastery of the aircraft in a steep turn?

    a) 40° to 50°.
    b) 45° to 90°.
    c) 20° to 30°.

15. The airspeed can increase or decrease as much as 10 knots without the examiner faulting the pilot for poor airspeed management.

    a) True.
    b) False.

16. If during a steep turn, the altitude was down 90 feet and then up by 40, would the private pilot candidate be considered to have performed within tolerances?

    a) Yes.
    b) No, because 90 feet exceeds acceptability standards.
    c) No, because 90 feet + 40 feet = 130 feet, which exceeds acceptability standards.

Answers to Study Questions

1. b
2. a
3. b
4. b
5. c
6. a
7. back elevator
8. a
9. b
10. ☒ Bank angle changes of 1° to 3°
    ☒ Increasing or relaxing back elevator pressure
    ☒ Coordinated use of aileron and rudder

11. c
12. clear the area
    power; airspeed
    instrument reference; reference
    other traffic
    entry; recovery
13. c
14. a
15. a (true)
16. a

Night Operations

Study Questions

1. Why does the area at the center of human vision become less effective at night?

    a) The portion of the brain responsible for vision goes to sleep at night.
    b) The eyelids become heavier at night and when tired, and reduce the field of vision.
    c) The process of night vision is placed almost entirely on the rods, which are concentrated in a ring around the cones.

2. How should a pilot consciously change their scanning technique at night or in low light conditions?

    a) Use off-center viewing.
    b) Move the eyes rapidly from side to side to detect movement.
    c) Stare directly at objects until the rods have time to absorb light.

3. After 5 to 10 minutes of darkness, human eyes become _____ times more sensitive to light than they were in a lighted area. After about 30 minutes, they are about _____ times more sensitive.

4. Fill in the blanks to show how a pilot can increase the effectiveness of night vision.

    *   Close _____ when exposed to bright light to avoid the blinding effect.
    *   Force the eyes to view _____.
    *   Avoid _____, drinking, and using _____ that may be harmful
    *   If _____ is available, use it during night flying.
    *   Move the eyes more _____ than in daylight.

5. At night, pilots should rely less on outside references because various distant lights and light patterns can confuse a pilot and indicate a

    a) false horizon.
    b) flock of birds.
    c) flying saucers.

6. Flicker vertigo can cause nausea, dizziness, headaches, or confusion, but can be eliminated or reduced by

    a) venting the cabin with fresh outside air.
    b) eliminating any light source causing blinking or flickering.
    c) approaching to land from a higher than normal altitude.

7. Altitude is more difficult to estimate visually at night, so pilots should rely on

   a) their kinesthetic sense of motion.
   b) the flight instruments and approach slope indicators if present.
   c) memory.

8. What are the two primary needs for personal flashlights?

   a) Preflight inspection and for signaling to the control tower in the event of radio failure.
   b) Visibility for cockpit operations, and for preflight inspection.
   c) To read charts in the cockpit, and increase the aircraft's visibility to other pilots.

9. Select the answers below that make the statements true.

   In preparing for a night flight, pilots often carry two / six types of flashlights. During preflight, a flashing / white light is used to examine the aircraft for airworthiness. In flight, a red light is used for signaling / cockpit operations. Use of the red light will not aid / impair night vision and will help the pilot retain dark adaptation / aggregation needed for viewing outside the aircraft. One downside of using red cockpit lighting is that aeronautical charts / beacons often show information in red which may be easy / hard to read if red cabin lighting is used.

10. Aircraft navigation lights match those used on water vessels. The right wingtip displays a steady _____ light, the left wingtip displays a steady _____ light, and the tail has a steady _____ light.

11. Some people have trouble remembering which color position light is on each wingtip. In each row, circle the words that meet the stated criteria.

    Has Fewer Letters?
               Red   or   Green
               Left   or   Right

    Has More Letters?
               Red   or   Green
               Left   or   Right

    Contains a "G"?
               Red   or   Green
               Left   or   Right

    Has a soft "e" sound, as in "led"?
               Red   or   Green
               Left   or   Right

12. In politics, red is often associated with communism and is on the left / right of the political continuum.

13. The two aircraft below are converging. Determine the color of each of the airplane's wingtip position lights.

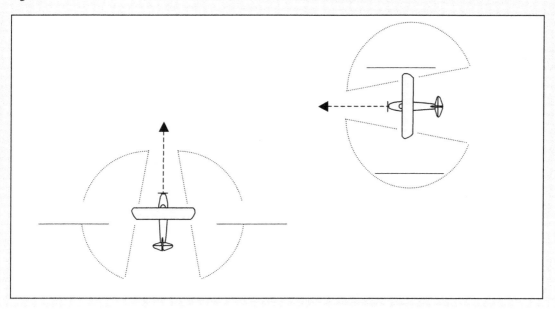

 14. Remember that when two aircraft are converging (other than when head-on), the aircraft on the right has the right of way. Which color light would the aircraft on the right see on the other traffic?

a) The pilot on the right would see the other aircraft's green light. Green meaning go.
b) The pilot on the right would see the other aircraft's red light to indicate that they have right of way.
c) The pilot on the right would see a flashing white light warning them to turn around.

15. The pilot safety program "Operation Lights ON" encourages pilots to

a) have landing lights on when operating within 10 miles of an airport, day or night.
b) restrict landing light usage to the last mile of final approach to avoid blinding other aircraft.
c) use landing lights on in the daytime to indicate a loss of radio communication.

16. Where can the availability and status of lighting systems for your destination airport be found?

a) In the Pilot's Operating Handbook (POH).
b) In the Aeronautical Information Manual (AIM).
c) On aeronautical charts and in the Airport/Facility Directory (A/FD).

17. Beacons that produce red flashes are used to indicate

a) airports used exclusively by the military.
b) obstructions or areas consider hazardous to aerial navigation.
c) the boundaries of restricted areas or military operation areas.

18. Which of the following are procedures that should be used during preflight preparation for a night flight? (Check all that apply.)

☐ Check flashlights to ensure they are operational
☐ Draw your course line on the chart in black ink
☐ Review available weather reports and forecasts, with special attention paid to indications of reduced visibility
☐ Identify lighted visual checkpoints along the route
☐ All interior and exterior aircraft lighting should be verified as operational
☐ Closely examine the parking area for chocks, chains, potholes, or obstructions

19. Why is it especially important to hold or lock the brakes during runup for night flights?

a) Lack of airflow over the wheels increases the chance of brake overheating.
b) Brake fluid cools at night and could possible drain from the system.
c) At night, it is more possible for the aircraft to creep forward without it being noticed.

20. The procedures for night takeoffs is the same as for normal daytime takeoffs except

a) that the airspeeds used are always 10 knots higher than in daytime.
b) that many of the runway visual cues are not available.
c) that flight instruments are not referenced as much so that attention can be put outside the aircraft.

21. If on a night flight, the pilot noticed that the lights on the surface were gradually disappearing, what might that indicate?

a) The airplane is flying into clouds or over a fog layer.
b) The airplane is flying higher than true altitude.
c) The pilot's eyes have not yet adapted to darkness.

22. Because of the loss of visual cues and the possibility for optical illusions, pilots should avoid

a) night flight.
b) crossing large bodies of water at night.
c) flight above 5,000 feet MSL.

23. When landing at night, the roundout and flare should begin

a) at a higher than normal altitude to allow the pilot's eyes to adjust.
b) when the landing lights reflect on the runway and tire marks on the runway can be clearly seen.
c) as soon as the pilot gets an on-glidepath indication from the VASI lights.

★ 24. Emergency landings done at night should be completed

a) in the same way as during the daytime, with an understanding that the pilot will have less ability to determine the safety of the landing site with certainty.
b) as quickly as possible.
c) as normally as possible, with the pilot selecting the most well-lit landing area possible.

Answers to Study Questions

1. c

2. a

3. 100
   100,000

4. one eye
   off center
   smoking; drugs
   supplemental oxygen
   slowly

5. a

6. b

7. b

8. b

9. two
   white
   cockpit
   impair
   adaptation
   charts
   hard

10. green
    red
    white

11. Red, Left   Green, Right
    Green, Right   Red, Left

12. left

13.

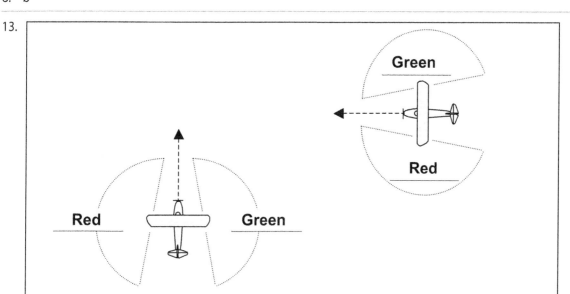

14. a

15. a

16. c

17. b

18. ☒ Check flashlights to ensure they are operational
    ☒ Draw your course line on the chart in black ink
    ☒ Review available weather reports and forecasts, with special attention paid to indications of reduced visibility
    ☒ Identify lighted visual checkpoints along the route
    ☒ All interior and exterior aircraft lighting should be verified as operational
    ☒ Closely examine the parking area for chocks, chains, potholes, or obstructions

19. c

20. b

21. a

22. b

23. b

24. a

Transition to Complex Airplanes

READING ASSIGNMENT

AFH Chapter 11 – *Transition to Complex Airplanes*

Study Questions

1. Complex airplanes are ones which have

   a) advanced computer based navigation systems.
   b) hard to read instrumentation and more than one control yoke.
   c) retractable landing gear, wing flaps, and a controllable-pitch propeller.

2. Flaps differ from ailerons in that the changes in lift created act

   a) symmetrically on the airplane.
   b) in the vertical axis.
   c) to create a rolling or yawing tendency.

 3. In flight situations in which additional lift is needed but airspeed needs to remain high, a pilot would be expected to use

   a) flaps of up to 15°.
   b) flaps of more than 15°.
   c) full flap deflection.

4. In flight situations in which the pilot was intentionally creating drag to help slow the aircraft, he or she would likely use

   a) no flaps.
   b) flaps of up to 15°.
   c) full flap deflection.

5. On a jumbo jet, passengers can watch the wing surface area radically increase as the plane prepares for landing. Flap panels that were hidden within the wing extend out and back a considerable distance. Sometimes similar panels extend forward from the leading edge of the wing. High-lift systems such as these are making use of

   a) split flaps.
   b) Fowler flaps.
   c) hidden/release flaps.

6. When a slotted flap is extended, the airplane

    a) has better takeoff and climb performance.
    b) will sink as the air escapes upward through the slot.
    c) will stall.

7. Which procedure facilitates a more stabilized approach?

    a) Large flap deflections at one single point in the landing pattern.
    b) Incremental deflection of flaps on downwind, base, and final approach.
    c) Neither. Operation of flaps has no impact on approach stability.

8. When landing in strong crosswinds, pilots can improve lateral control by

    a) using full extension of flaps.
    b) limiting the amount of flaps used.
    c) reducing positive control of the rudder pedals.

9. In executing a go around, the desire to eliminate excess drag by retracting flaps should be carefully balanced against

    a) the possibility of the aircraft sinking back to the runway from loss of lift.
    b) the strong nose down tendency that results from full power application.
    c) the need to maintain drag in the climb.

10. Why does the need arise for controllable-pitch propellers?

    a) A fixed pitch propeller is like a plain donut. Pilots need challenge and desire variety.
    b) A fixed pitch propeller is like a bike with only one gear – hard to start moving and then limited in speed by how fast your legs can move. We get better efficiency at both low speeds and high speeds if we can adjust the pitch angle appropriately at different airspeeds.
    c) A fixed pitch propeller is solid metal, and very heavy. Controllable-pitch propellers are hollow and result in less weight on the airframe.

11. A constant-speed propeller is one type of controllable-pitch propeller. In a constant-speed propeller the pilot does not directly control the pitch angle of the propeller, but instead sets a desired r.p.m. using

    the propeller control knob and relies on a _____ that is geared to the crankshaft to adjust the propeller pitch angle until that r.p.m. is reached.

12. Pulling back (aft) on the propeller control knob causes the

    a) propeller blades to move to a higher angle of attack.
    b) propeller blades to move to a lower angle of attack.
    c) engine power to reduce to idle.

13. Pushing forward on the propeller control results in high / low r.p.m. and high / low blade pitch.

14. For takeoff and climb, the propeller should be set for

    a) high r.p.m. and high pitch.
    b) low r.p.m. and low pitch.
    c) high r.p.m. and low pitch.

15. In one type of constant-speed propeller system, oil from the engine is pumped into the propeller hub causing the propeller blades to twist to a higher blade angle. When oil flows outward from the propeller back to the engine, springs in the propeller hub return the blade angle to flat pitch. In this type of system, a catastrophic loss of engine oil would result in

    a) the propeller blades moving to a higher angle of attack.
    b) the propeller blades moving to a lower angle of attack.
    c) the propeller blades frozen at their current pitch.

16. During preflight testing of the powerplant, the propeller control should be cycled momentarily from flat pitch to high pitch to test that the system works correctly and to

    a) circulate fresh warm oil through the propeller governor system.
    b) alert other pilots to the equipment capabilities onboard your aircraft.
    c) allow the electrical power to reach the alternator.

There is a definite order of operations for the pilot to use when increasing or decreasing power output from the engine in order to minimize stress on the engine and propeller. The diagram below shows the standard arrangement of engine power controls (or "power stack") for an airplane equipped with a constant-speed propeller.

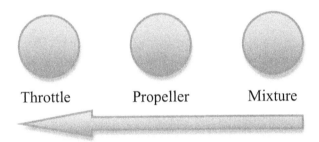

17. When powering up for takeoff or to begin a climb, the pilot should advance the controls forward one at a time, moving from right to left across the power stack. This protects the powerplant by

    a) increasing propeller pitch (and drag) before increasing engine power.
    b) decreasing the propeller pitch (and drag) before increasing engine power.
    c) decreasing the richness of the mixture before opening the throttle.

18. Select the answers below that make the statements true.

High stress within the engine can result when engine manifold pressure is high (engine forcing the propeller to spin faster) and the propeller control set to high / low r.p.m. (governor trying to slow propeller down by increasing / decreasing blade angle.)

This situation can be avoided if the pilot follows a standard procedure for increasing and decreasing power output. When increasing power, increase the r.p.m. first / last . When decreasing power, apply the controls in the same / opposite direction.

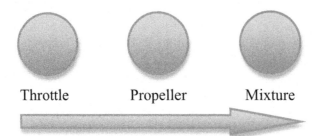

Throttle   Propeller   Mixture

19. In the diagram above, the arrows represents the pilot adjusting the control settings left to right. This method is used to

   a) power up, like when initiating a climb.
   b) power back, like when leveling out from a climb.
   c) in all power change situations.

20. The manifold pressure value (in inches Hg) should never exceed the r.p.m. value (in hundreds of r.p.m.) in normally aspirated engines.

   a) True.
   b) False.

21. The key operating principle of a turbocharger is to use exhausts gases to power an air compressor that

   a) increases the speed and lowers the pressure of air flowing into the engine cylinders.
   b) heats the air in advance of combustion, richening the mixture.
   c) increases the density of the air available for combustion.

22. When operating a turbocharged airplane, all movements of the power controls should be

   a) slow and gentle.
   b) abrupt and dramatic.
   c) in a clockwise manner.

23. One reason that turbocharged engines run at higher operating temperatures than non-turbocharged engines is

   a) the air inbound to the engine is heated as a byproduct of the process of compressing it.
   b) turbocharged engines are usually operated at lower power settings.
   c) the air inbound to the engine is intentionally heated to increase its density.

24. The primary benefits of being able to retract the landing gear of an airplane are _____ climb performance and _____ cruise airspeeds.

25. In most airplanes with retractable gear, the gear switch on the control panel is shaped like a _____ in order to facilitate positive identification and to differentiate it from other cockpit controls.

   a) blade.
   b) hook.
   c) wheel.

26. Landing gear position lights on the panel will confirm when the landing gear are up or down. Why are these lights usually of the "press to test" type, and often have interchangeable bulbs?

    a) To allow the copilot to create interest light patterns with bulbs of different colors.
    b) For cost efficiency.
    c) The pilot must be able to distinguish between a serious landing gear malfunction and a simple light bulb burning out.

27. A squat switch helps prevent against accidental landing gear retraction while on the ground by

    a) forcing the pilot to use pressure from both knees simultaneously on sensors in the cockpit to operate the landing gear system.
    b) using the weight of the airplane to open circuits preventing gear retraction.
    c) using infrared signals to sense height above the ground.

28. Preflight inspection of an airplane equipped with retractable landing gear should include

    a) close inspection of landing gear position indicators in the cockpit and external inspection of the individual system components.
    b) test retraction on the gear while parked in the tie-down area.
    c) a test bleed of the hydraulic system to check color of fluid.

29. The landing gear should not be retracted until

    a) pattern altitude.
    b) reaching the midpoint distance of the takeoff runway.
    c) a positive rate of climb is indicated on the flight instruments.

Answers to Study Questions

1. c
2. a
3. a
4. c
5. b
6. a
7. b
8. b
9. a
10. b
11. propeller governor
12. a
13. high; low
14. c
15. b
16. a

17. b
18. low
    increasing
    first
    opposite
19. b
20. b (false)
21. c
22. a
23. a
24. increased
    higher
25. c
26. c
27. b
28. a
29. c

Transition to Tailwheel Airplanes

READING ASSIGNMENT
AFH Chapter 13 – *Transition to Tailwheel Airplanes*

Study Questions

1. Why do you think tailwheel airplanes are often referred to as "conventional gear" airplanes?

   a) Tailwheel pilots often meet up at flying conventions.
   b) Tailwheel pilots tend to be more conservative flyers.
   c) Historically, this was the first landing gear configuration and was the standard convention for many years. Nosewheel aircraft were designed later.

2. A key aerodynamic difference in a tailwheel aircraft is that the airplane's center of gravity (CG) is located

   a) in front of the main landing gear.
   b) behind the main landing gear.
   c) in advance of the propeller.

3. When applying brakes in a tailwheel aircraft, brakes must be applied

   a) firmly, and fully.
   b) smoothly, evenly, and cautiously.
   c) in short bursts.

4. When taxiing a tailwheel aircraft in moderate to strong headwinds, the elevator control

   a) becomes less effective.
   b) should be held aft to hold the elevator up and the tail down.
   c) is used for directional control down the taxiway.

5. If the engine cowling is high enough to restrict the pilot's vision of the area directly in front of the airplane, the pilot should

   a) stand up higher in the cockpit to maintain visual contact forward.
   b) abandon the flight.
   c) taxi in a zigzag fashion, with a series of short s-turns.

6. With the CG aft of the main wheels, the mass of the aircraft acts as if it is pushing the main wheels forward. How does that impact directional control?

   a) Directional control is very stable, and only passive rudder control is needed.
   b) Directional control is very unstable, and slight changes in the yaw position of the airplane on the takeoff or landing roll can, if not corrected, exaggerate themselves into a ground loop.
   c) Directional control is difficult as the weight makes the rudder pedals heavy and difficult to move.

7. Rudder pressure must be used _____ to counteract yawing forces so the airplane continues straight down the runway.

    a) promptly and smoothly.
    b) sparingly.
    c) in combination with firm, positive brake pressure.

8. During the early portion of the takeoff roll, the tail of a tailwheel airplane should

    a) rise off the ground slightly to permit the airplane to accelerate more rapidly.
    b) wag from side to side until a neutral position naturally establishes itself.
    c) be held firmly to the ground as long as possible.

9. While watching a tailwheel airplane takeoff during strong crosswinds, you observe the downwind wing rise and the downwind main wheel lift off the runway, with the remainder of the takeoff roll being made on one wheel. The pilot has

    a) mismanaged the takeoff and is side-skipping.
    b) lost directional control of the aircraft.
    c) taken off perfectly into a sideslip.

10. Soft-field takeoff procedures in a tailwheel aircraft

    a) differ sharply from those for nosewheel aircraft.
    b) are essentially the same as those for nosewheel aircraft.
    c) require full forward application of the elevator control to keep pressure on the main gear.

11. A critical aspect of tailwheel landing is for the elevator control to be carefully eased fully back after ground contact, to keep the tailwheel on the ground and to prevent

    a) the airplane from nosing over.
    b) the elevator control stick from contacting the instrument panel.
    c) an increase in pitch attitude.

12. Any loss of directional control on the landing roll may lead to

    a) an aggravated, uncontrolled, tight turn on the ground (or "ground loop").
    b) loss of engine power.
    c) sanctions by the Federal Aviation Administration.

13. Why are tailwheel aircraft characteristically prone to weathervaning in a strong crosswind?

    a) The small size of the tailwheel means insufficient weight to hold the plane stable.
    b) The airplane has a much greater side profile behind main gear for the wind to hit and pivot the plane around.
    c) The downwind wing has a high likelihood of raising up into the wind and limiting directional control.

14. To execute a wheel landing, the pilot first holds the airplane in a level flight attitude until the main wheels touch, then

    a) pushes forward on the stick.
    b) increases engine power.
    c) immediately and smoothly reduces throttle and holds sufficient forward elevator to hold the main wheels on the ground.

 15. Some of the same forces that cause an airplane to ground loop can be seen in

    a) a car driving forward at high speed and suddenly skidding to a stop.
    b) a car driving quickly in reverse and losing directional control.
    c) skidding on ice on a frozen road.

FTW-13

Answers to Study Questions

1. c
2. b
3. b
4. b
5. c
6. b
7. a
8. a

9. c
10. b
11. a
12. a
13. b
14. c
15. b

Emergency Landings

READING ASSIGNMENT
AFH Pages 16-1 to 16-7 – "Emergency Situations" through "Emergency Descents"

Study Questions

1. What or who is the ultimate authority in what procedures to be used in the event of an inflight emergency?

   a) The Airplane Flying Handbook.
   b) The designated FAA-examiner.
   c) The pilot operating handbook (POH) for that aircraft.

2. Define the following terms:

   forced landing   _____

   precautionary landing   _____

   ditching   _____

3. What could cause a pilot to decide not to make a precautionary landing when one is advisable or necessary?

   a) Wishful thinking.
   b) Emergency procedures in the POH.
   c) Lack of a certificate or rating.

4. What is one way that a pilot's reluctance to accept an emergency situation can result in an avoidable tragedy?

   a) Prompt establishment of gliding airspeed can result in an avoidable delay in the descent.
   b) An unconscious desire to avoid the dreaded moment may lead to a delay in the selection of an appropriate emergency landing area.
   c) Planning the approach off airport can unnecessarily delay the pilot's ability to correctly reestablish fuel flow to the engine.

5. Select the answers below that make the statements true.

    In some situations, the pilot could unintentionally <u>increase / decrease</u> the danger to himself and his passengers by placing too <u>little / much</u> emphasis on trying to save the aircraft from damage. Simulated <u>forced / short-field</u> landing practice only in areas with safe landing <u>procedures / areas</u> could lead the pilot to try to avoid touchdown in terrain where airplane damage is <u>unexpected / unavoidable</u> . Examples of this include attempting an impossible turn back to the runway with insufficient <u>altitude / airspeed</u> , or choosing a landing area that affords no margin for error.

    Two factors that can increase this error are the pilot's <u>financial stake / prior time</u> in the aircraft, and the belief that an undamaged airplane implies no bodily harm. There are times, however, when the pilot should choose to <u>defend / sacrifice</u> the airplane so that the occupants can safely walk away from the landing.

6. Avoidance of crash injuries is largely a matter of

    a) protecting the wings and flight control surfaces from damage or impact.
    b) keeping the vital structure of the aircraft relatively intact by using dispensable structure such as wings and landing gear to absorb the violence of the stopping process.
    c) choosing to make sudden stops instead of prolonging the deceleration process during an off-airport landing.

7. Why are seat belts and shoulder straps critical to maintaining bodily security in the event of a forced landing?

    a) The human body must be decelerated at the same rate as the surrounding fuselage in order to benefit from the fuselage's relative intactness.
    b) Seat belts and shoulder harnesses provide a psychological feeling of safety and security.
    c) The seat belts are made of material that will yield during landings in which it is safer for the body to be thrown free of the airplane.

8. What are examples of things that should be used to absorb the energy of the aircraft in a crash landing?

    a) The fuselage.
    b) Small trees, cultivated crops, and brush.
    c) Rocks, or craggy mountainous outcroppings.

9. It is important that the actual touchdown during an emergency landing be made at the lowest possible controllable _____ using all available aerodynamic devices.

10. In general, which of the following would be the best attitude for the airplane in execution of an emergency landing?

    a) Nose-low pitch attitude.
    b) Steep bank angles.
    c) Wings level, nose level (or slightly high).

11. What should be the ideal vertical sink rate on touchdown in an emergency landing?

   a)   A flat touchdown with a high sink rate to provide greater surface friction and deceleration.
   b)   High sink rates, but only on soft terrain; otherwise, low sink rates.
   c)   A minimal sink rate at touchdown is preferable.

12. A well-executed crash landing in poor terrain can be less hazardous than

   a)   a well-executed normal landing on an established field.
   b)   an uncontrolled touchdown on an established field.
   c)   a soft-field landing on a dirt runway.

13. What is true of use of flaps during final approach in an emergency landing?

   a)   Flaps should be deployed as early in the approach as possible to increase drag and slow the aircraft.
   b)   Flaps should never be used in an emergency landing.
   c)   Flaps should be used to improve maneuverability at slow airspeeds, but pilots should exercise caution in the timing and extent of their application.

 14. What advantage of the use of flaps in a normal landing can create a hazard in an engine-out, emergency landing if not properly managed?

   a)   Increased angle of descent.
   b)   Increased airspeed on final approach.
   c)   Reduced deceleration as a result of aerodynamic drag.

15. Why might a gear-up landing on a plowed field result in less damage to the aircraft than a gear-down landing?

   a)   The plowed furrows can raise the nose of the airplane and prevent the propeller from striking the surface.
   b)   Landing gear are less able to support the weight of the aircraft than the bottom of the fuselage.
   c)   Landing gear could catch unevenly and flip the aircraft, and collapsed landing gear can contribute to fuel tank rupture.

16. How should a pilot of an irregularly running engine manage the engine operation in a forced landing?

   a)   Unless the engine is operating fully, it should be shut down at the first indication that an emergency landing is imminent.
   b)   Any engine power is better than no engine power, so leave it running.
   c)   Leave it running on approach, and shut it off just prior to landing.

17. Experience shows that a collision with ground obstacles at the end of a ground roll, is much less hazardous than striking an obstacle before the touchdown point is reached.

   a)   True.
   b)   False.

18. Why would a river or creek be an inviting alternative for an emergency landing?

   a)   The riverbed is often relatively level, soft ground with open area above.
   b)   Water decelerates the airplane faster than landing on dry pavement.
   c)   The water can be used to wash the airplane after the crash landing.

19. Why should a pilot making an emergency landing on a road or across a road be on heightened alert?

_____

_____

_____

20. When making a landing into trees, the pilot should try to "hang" the airplane in the tree branches by

   a) making a slightly faster than normal approach and keeping the nose level or slightly down.
   b) using the fuselage to absorb the main impact and protecting the wings for flight.
   c) keeping the groundspeed as low as possible and keeping the nose high.

21. What can result when landing on snow or ditching over a wide expanse of smooth water?

   a) Loss of depth perception and errors in landing.
   b) Increased visibility.
   c) Loss of rudder effectiveness.

22. On takeoff, when altitudes are below 500 feet AGL, an engine failure should result in the pilot

   a) making a 180° turn back to the runway.
   b) establishing the proper glide attitude, and landing directly ahead or slightly to either side of the takeoff path.
   c) making a slight turn downwind to gain airspeed for landing.

23. The goal of an emergency descent is to

   a) maintain altitude for as long as possible.
   b) lose altitude as rapidly as possible.
   c) glide the farthest distance possible.

24. Name a situation that would demand an emergency descent.

_____

_____

 25. Why are simulated emergency descents made in a turn?

   a) To minimize load factor on the airframe.
   b) To improve radio reception.
   c) To check for other air traffic below and to look for possible landing areas (and reduce the vertical component of lift for a faster descent).

26. Except when prohibited by the aircraft manufacturer, the power setting in an emergency descent should be

   a) full throttle.
   b) normal power setting for high-speed cruise flight.
   c) idle.

27. The airspeed selected for emergency descent should be

    a) V_A.

    b) V_{LE}.

    c) the maximum allowable airspeed consistent with the aircraft configuration and air conditions.

28. Why would a pilot choose a high airspeed emergency descent in the event of an engine fire?

    a) The increased airflow might blow out the fire.

    b) The increased nose-down attitude will protect the cabin from spread of the fire.

    c) High airspeed descents should NEVER be used in the event of an engine fire.

Answers to Study Questions

1. c

2. An immediate landing necessitated by the inability to continue further flight
A premeditated landing when further flight is possible, but inadvisable
A forced or precautionary landing on water

3. a

4. b

5. increase
much
forced
areas
unavoidable
altitude
financial stake
sacrifice

6. b

7. a

8. b

9. airspeed

10. c

11. c

12. b

13. c

14. a

15. c

16. c

17. a (true)

18. a

19. Manmade obstacles, such as power or telephone lines and support structures, can be on either side of a road and many not be visible until the final portion of the approach.

20. c

21. a

22. b

23. b

24. fire, sudden loss of cabin pressurization, or any other situation in which the aircraft must be on the ground as soon as possible

25. c

26. c

27. c

28. a

In-Flight Fires and Systems Malfunctions

Study Questions

Page 16-7 – In-flight Fire

1. How can a pilot prepare to deal with fires in flight?

   a) Memorizing the steps outlined in the Airplane Flying Handbook.
   b) Becoming familiar with the procedures outlined in the AFM/POH for the particular airplane.
   c) By setting small, controllable, practice fires while in flight in isolated practice areas.

2. An in-flight fire in the engine compartment is usually caused by a flammable substance such as
   _____ coming into contact with a hot surface.

3. What are the most obvious indication of engine compartment fires?

   a) Fire alarm indicator light flashing on the control panel.
   b) Smoke and/or flames coming from the engine cowling area.
   c) Exhaust odors entering the cabin.

4. Other, less obvious indications of engine fires can be discoloration, bubbling, or melting of the

   a) fuel lines or hoses.
   b) propeller.
   c) engine cowling skin.

5. Most of the time, a pilot will become aware of an engine fire long before the fire develops into a real danger.

   a) True.
   b) False.

6. In general, the first step on discovering an engine fire is to shut off the _____ to the engine.

   a) fuel supply
   b) air supply
   c) ignition spark

7. Each airplane is different, but some basic similarities exist. Name some ways to cut fuel flow to the engine.

   _____

   _____

   _____

8. How should the ignition switch be positioned to deal with an engine fire in flight, and why?

   _____

   _____

   _____

   _____

9. When should the engine be restarted when dealing with an engine fire in flight?

   a) Once all of the initial fuel has been exhausted and the fire is out.
   b) No sooner than 10 minutes after last of the smoke or flames are visible.
   c) It should not be restarted. The pilot should prepare for an engine out landing.

10. Why is it beneficial to stop the propeller from spinning in response to an oil fire?

   a) To allow the pilot better forward visibility.
   b) To allow more air to flow directly into the cowling to blow out the fire.
   c) To stop engine-driven oil pumps from adding more oil to the fire.

11. What factor should the pilot consider when deciding whether to shut off the master electrical switch during an engine fire?

   a) Electricity from the system could allow the engine fire to spread into the cabin.
   b) Deactivating the electrical system prevents the use of panel radios for transmitting distress messages and transponder signals.
   c) Disabling the electrical system can prevent sparks in the cylinder and may extinguish the fire.

12. What is true of the value of the airplane and its occupants?

   a) It is always worth it to fly farther to get the airplane to a hard surface runway, so that landing damage to the aircraft can be minimized.
   b) The largest losses associated with in-flight fires are the cost of the damage to the airframe and powerplant.
   c) The airplane is expendable and the only thing that matters is the safety of those on board.

13. What is characteristic of electrical fires?

   a) The panel lights flicker but continue to work.
   b) The distinct odor of burning electrical insulation.
   c) The engine oil temperature gauge will continue to operate even when the entire electrical system has been shut down.

14. Which is the most cautious approach to dealing with in-flight electrical fires?

    a) Slowly and meticulously attempting to identify the faulty circuit, and then only if necessary, shutting off the entire electrical system.
    b) Shutting off the entire electrical system first, and if flight conditions permit, bringing the most needed items online one at a time to attempt to isolate the faulty circuit.
    c) Leaning the fuel mixture, and being ready to shutdown the engine if necessary.

15. As with other fires, what is the most prudent course of action in dealing with electrical fires?

    a) Land as soon as possible.
    b) Land at the nearest airport with maintenance facilities.
    c) Return to the airport of origin and have the aircraft inspected by a certificated aviation mechanic.

16. What two immediate demands must be dealt with by the pilot in the event of a cabin fire?

    _____

    _____

17. In what order are the windows opened and the fire extinguisher used to combat cabin fires in flight?

    a) Open the windows, then use the fire extinguisher.
    b) Use the fire extinguisher, then open the windows.
    c) There is no logical reason to prefer one way or the other.

18. A pilot can attempt to expel smoke from the cabin by opening windows or vents, but they should be closed again immediately if

    a) the outside air temperature is below freezing.
    b) the fire becomes more intense.
    c) there is visible moisture in the air.

19. How could lowering the landing gear or flaps aggravate a cabin smoke problem?

    a) Lowering the landing gear allows air to force its way into the cabin through the landing gear wheel wells.
    b) Lowering of gear and flaps can alter the airflow pattern around the wings and limit the ability to vent the cabin.
    c) The flaps or gear control levers can overheat and contribute to the fire.

20. A no-flap landing can increase the required landing distance on the runway by as much as

    _____

21. Due to the loss of drag associated with flaps, in a no-flap landing what method of losing altitude should NOT be used?

    a) Slipping the aircraft.
    b) Diving (nosing down).
    c) Flying at a slightly nose-high attitude.

22. When landing without flaps, the danger exists that the pilot may attempt to

    a) land with cross-controls to increase forward visibility.
    b) flare too high above the runway for too long, resulting in a drop.
    c) force the airplane onto the runway at an excessively high speed.

23. What could result from flaring too excessively in a no-flap landing?

    a) The tail of the aircraft striking the runway.
    b) Landing flat with too much weight on the nosewheel.
    c) Excess engine power on rollout.

24. What is an asymmetric flap situation?

    a) When one of the flap surfaces splits in flight, allowing the pilot to control each side individually.
    b) Airplanes equipped with Fowler flaps that retract up and into the wing are known as "asymmetric" flaps.
    c) When one flap retracts or extends and the other does not.

25. A real spin danger exists in a split flap landing because

    a) the aircraft will tend to roll toward the wing with the most flap deflection.
    b) each wing has a different stall speed and strong yaw moments exist.
    c) Airplanes equipped with split flaps are designed for aerobatics and are built to endure high wing loading.

26. The landing approach when landing with a split flap condition should be flown at

    a) lower than normal airspeed.
    b) normal airspeed.
    c) higher than normal airspeed.

27. If one of the two elevator control cables breaks in flight, the pilot should use trim control

    a) for pitch control instead of yoke/elevator movements.
    b) by applying considerable trim in the direction of the lost elevator control cable, and manage pitch with increasing or relaxing the opposing elevator pressure.
    c) sparingly, so as not to exacerbate the problem.

28. If the elevator becomes jammed and will not move, the pilot must be adept at using _____ to maintain limited pitch control.

    a) coordinated aileron and rudder movement
    b) airspeed and cabin weight shifts
    c) power settings and flap extension

29. In the event of an alternator or generator failure, it is essential that the pilot immediately shed non-essential _____, notify _____ of the situation, and then plan to land at the nearest suitable _____.

30. What should a pilot expect when landing with a complete electrical system failure in an aircraft that has electrically controlled landing gear and flap extension motors?

 a) The pilot should extend gear and flaps immediately while still enroute to ensure they are out when needed at landing.
 b) The pilot should expect to make a no-flap landing and anticipate extending the landing gear using the manual extension lever.
 c) Given a choice, the pilot would choose to extend flaps and ask the airport to foam the runway for a gear up landing.

31. (Refer to AFH, Figure 16-9) Other than the starter motor, what device typically consumes the most electrical energy?

_____

32. Which takes more power to operate, radio receivers or radio transmitters (transceivers)?

 a) Once the radio is powered on, the energy draw is the same for listening or transmitting.
 b) Receivers take more energy because they have to listen farther.
 c) It takes more energy to transmit than to receive.

33. From Table 1, how serious would you say it is if the oil pressure is indicating either above or below the normal operating limitations on the oil pressure gauge?

 a) Not that serious, the airplane should just be given more warmup time.
 b) Very serious, and pilot should land as soon as possible.
 c) Only serious if the engine oil temperature is also indicating beyond operating limits.

34. What are some ways to cool the engine if cylinder head temperatures are too high?

_____

_____

_____

35. What should the pilot try if the fuel pressure is reading unusually low in flight?

 a) Reduce power and feather the propeller.
 b) Open cowl flaps and enrich fuel mixture to the engine.
 c) Check fuel selector switch, fuel tanks, fuel cutoff valve, and turn on auxiliary fuel pump.

36. What is the proper response if a door comes open during flight?

 a) Relax and concentrate on flying the airplane. Make sure everyone has their seatbelt on.
 b) Try to slip the airplane towards the door to push it closed.
 c) Close the door immediately, before the roll and/or yaw effects are allowed to develop into a dangerous flight condition.

Answers to Study Questions

1. b
2. fuel, oil, or hydraulic fluid
3. b
4. c
5. b (false)
6. a
7. fuel cutoff valve, fuel selector valve, mixture control to cutoff
8. The ignition switch be left on in order to use up the fuel that remains in the fuel lines and components between the fuel selector/shutoff valve and the engine.
9. c
10. c
11. b
12. c
13. b
14. b
15. a
16. (1) Attack the fire. (2) Get the airplane safely on the ground as quickly as possible.
17. b
18. b
19. b
20. 50%
21. b
22. c
23. a
24. c
25. b
26. c
27. b
28. c
29. non-essential electrical loads
    ATC
    airport
30. b
31. landing lights
32. c
33. b
34. opening cowl flaps, increasing airspeed, making the fuel mixture more rich, and reducing power
35. c
36. a

Inadvertent VFR Flight into IMC

READING ASSIGNMENT

AFH Pages 16-12 to 16-17 – "Inadvertent VFR Flight into IMC" through "Transition to Visual Flight"

Study Questions

1. Which answer best describes when a VFR pilot is said to be in instrument meteorological conditions (IMC)?

    a) Anytime the aircraft is surrounded by clouds at or below 1,000 feet AGL.
    b) Anytime the pilot is unable to maintain airplane attitude control by reference to the natural horizon.
    c) Anytime the in flight visibility is below 3 statute miles.

2. The inability to navigate or establish geographical position by visual reference to landmarks on the surface

    a) should be accepted by the pilot as a genuine emergency, requiring appropriate action.
    b) is normal, provided the pilot is flying in an aircraft certified for IFR operation.
    c) is of minor concern to a VFR pilot.

3. VFR pilots should understand that without appropriate _____, qualification, and recent flight experience in the control of an airplane solely by reference to flight _____, they will be unable to do so for any _____ of time.

4. If the natural horizon were to suddenly disappear, the untrained instrument pilot would be subject to

    a) updrafts and minor turbulence.
    b) vertigo, spatial disorientation, and inevitable loss of airplane control.
    c) engine and radio communication systems failures.

5. The most important point to be stressed for VFR pilots encountering instrument meteorological conditions is that the pilot

    a) should panic.
    b) may panic if they so choose.
    c) must not panic.

6. The single biggest contribution a VFR pilot can make to his or her own safety if the airplane suddenly flies into a cloud is to

    a) become overwhelmed and apprehensive.
    b) make sudden large control movements to find a way out of the cloud.
    c) make a conscious effort to relax and to not panic.

7. After inadvertently entering into a cloud and not panicking, a VFR pilot's immediate and only concern should be to

   a) keep the wings level.
   b) attempt to descend below the cloud.
   c) lowering the head to look for the appropriate VFR chart.

8. Vibrations from the airplane can create false sensations in the inner ear that may fool the pilot into believing something wrong about the attitude of the airplane. The best way to avoid this sort of spatial disorientation is to

   a) believe what the flight instruments show regardless of what the natural senses tell.
   b) tilt the head from one side to the other to "reset" the sense of balance and inertia.
   c) close the eyes and use fingertip control pressures to sense the attitude of the airplane.

9. The primary instrument for attitude control is the

   a) heading indicator.
   b) altimeter.
   c) attitude indicator.

10. During flight in IMC, any pitch changes should be made by using no more than _____ up or down change in the attitude indicator.

    a) one bar width.
    b) 5°.
    c) 10°.

11. Turns by instrument reference must be made with extreme caution as a strong potential exists for the pilot to overcontrol the airplane, which could result in

    a) an excessively steep bank and instability.
    b) an inability to move the airplane from straight and level flight.
    c) damage to the flight instruments.

12. Because the pilot should use only the lightest of touch to control the airplane while flying in IMC, it is especially important to keep the airplane

    a) properly trimmed.
    b) at full power.
    c) leaned to minimum fuel flow.

13. Descents made while flying in IMC should never been faster than

    a) 80 kts.
    b) 500 fpm.
    c) 2,100 rpm.

14. For the untrained instrument pilot, combined maneuvers, such as climbing or descending turns, should be

    a) performed quickly to get them over with.
    b) avoided if at all possible.
    c) performed at maximum power.

15. Why might a VFR pilot, having successfully flown back out of the clouds to an airport for landing, decide to circle the airport or wait a bit before landing?

    a) To follow general instrument flight rules, which require circling the airport once before landing.
    b) To allow time to become acclimatized again to VFR flight and oriented to the airport before attempting the landing.
    c) To survey the area and look for other areas of possible instrument conditions.

FTW-16C

Answers to Study Questions

1. b
2. a
3. training
   instruments
   length
4. b
5. c
6. c
7. a

8. a
9. c
10. a
11. a
12. a
13. b
14. b
15. b

Recovery from Unusual Attitude

READING ASSIGNMENT
**Instrument Flying Handbook (IFH) Pages 5-26 to 5-29 – "Unusual Attitudes and
Recoveries" through "Common Errors in Unusual Attitudes
PTS IX.E – Recovery from Unusual Flight Attitudes**

Study Questions

**Instrument Flying Handbook (IFH) Pages 5-26 to 5-29 – "Unusual Attitudes and
Recoveries" through "Common Errors in Unusual Attitudes**

1. An "unusual" attitude is a pitch attitude and/or bank attitude that

   a) happens only once every two years.
   b) is different than what other pilots are doing.
   c) is not normally required for normal (or instrument) flight.

2. In which of the following situations would you think a VFR pilot would be most likely to end up in an unusual attitude?

   a) Unexpected flight into weather conditions that limit visibility.
   b) Turning from base onto final at an unfamiliar airport.
   c) During ground reference maneuvers below 1,000 feet AGL with a strong crosswind.

3. How would a pilot be able to detect that the aircraft was at an unusual attitude without using the natural horizon as reference?

   a) By cross-checking the flight instruments.
   b) An unusual attitude warning light will illuminate on the annunciator panel.
   c) The airplane's bank alert warning horn will sound.

4. When a pilot notices that the aircraft is in an unusual attitude, the immediate problem is not how the airplane got there, but what it is doing and how to

   _____

   _____

5. The most important determination to be made quickly by a pilot in an unusual attitude is whether the airplane is

   a) nose high or nose low.
   b) wings level or banked.
   c) at high power or low power.

Recovery from Unusual Attitude

6. Why is the attitude indicator not the best source of information about extreme flight attitudes?

    a) The aircraft electrical system cannot correct for extreme bank or pitch attitudes.
    b) Sudden changes in air pressure can invalidate instrument readings.
    c) The indicator is very hard to interpret in extreme attitudes, and may be inoperative or spilled (exceeded its upset limits).

7. If the airspeed is decreasing, or below the desired airspeed, the pilot can deduce that the aircraft is in a nose-_____ attitude and power should be _____ as necessary in proportion to the observed deceleration.

8. The corrective control applications to recover from an unusual attitude are made almost simultaneously, but

    a) performing them in the proper sequence will make for a faster, safer recovery, and shows good understanding of the flight situation the aircraft is experiencing.
    b) the order can vary depending on the altitude at which the aircraft is flying.
    c) return to straight and level flight cannot be determined through use of the instruments.

9. After applying power to recover from a nose-high unusual attitude, the pilot immediately

    a) applies forward-elevator pressure to lower the nose, and uses coordinate aileron and rudder pressure to level the wings.
    b) sets the transponder code to 7-5-0-0 and contacts air traffic control for help.
    c) levels the wings and then pitches forward to regain airspeed.

10. A nose-high unusual attitude, if left uncorrected, could result in

    a) a spiral.
    b) a stall.
    c) a propeller overspeed.

11. Which of the following would be positive instrument indications of a nose-low unusual attitude? (Check all that apply.)

    ☐ Airspeed decreasing steadily
    ☐ Decreasing altitude
    ☐ VSI steady or indicating slight climb
    ☐ Airspeed increasing or above the desired airspeed
    ☐ Turn coordinator airplane banked to one side or the other
    ☐ Attitude indicator tumbled (or "spilled")

12. Once a nose-low attitude has been identified, the pilot should immediately

    a) add power.
    b) increase airspeed.
    c) decrease power.

13. A nose-low unusual attitude, if left uncorrected, could result in

    a) a stall, accelerated stall, or spin.
    b) excessive airspeed and loss of altitude.
    c) damage to the airspeed indicator.

14. Why do you think the wings are leveled before the nose is raised while recovering from a nose-low unusual attitude?

    a) To increase the vertical component of lift and therefore the effectiveness of the angle of attack increase.
    b) So that one wing is not lower to the ground, risking premature ground contact.
    c) To raise the stall speed and increase the margin of safety.

15. Unfortunately, once a nose-down unusual attitude has been detected, what is the instinctive reaction of most pilots?

    a) To immediate add power.
    b) To immediately level the wings.
    c) To immediately pull back on the elevator control first.

16. In the spaces provided, fill in the blanks to show the correct control adjustment. Use either Pitch, Power, or Bank.

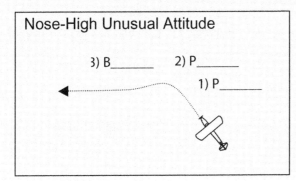 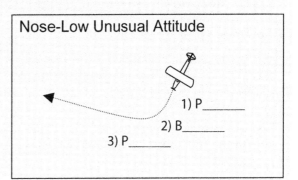

17. What is the indication on the altimeter when the aircraft has sufficiently recovered from a nose-low unusual attitude?

    a) The needle will indicate a stabilized descent.
    b) The needle will slow its descent, stop, and then reverse direction to show a climb.
    c) The needle will pass through the minimum safe altitude.

18. Why is coordinated use of the rudder so important when leveling the wings from a banked unusual attitude?

    a) Coordination increases drag and can aid in slowing the aircraft in a climb.
    b) Skidding or slipping sensations can easily aggravate disorientation and slow recovery.
    c) Only the rudder can keep the aircraft on the assigned course at the assigned altitude.

19. Attempting to recover by sensory sensations other than the view of the flight instruments can

    a) help the pilot to make a faster recovery.
    b) aid in rudder coordination.
    c) interfere with the correct control responses, as the other senses can easily be fooled or disoriented by flight conditions.

20. _____ is the impulse to stop and stare at one of the instruments once an instrument discrepancy has been noted, which interferes with the instrument cross-check.

 21. "Power – Pitch – Bank" would be the correct recovery sequence for

    a) a nose-high unusual attitude.
    b) a nose-low unusual attitude.
    c) any unusual attitude.

22. "Power – Bank – Pitch" would be the correct recovery sequence for

    a) a nose-high unusual attitude.
    b) a nose-low unusual attitude.
    c) any unusual attitude.

PTS IX.E – Recovery from Unusual Flight Attitudes

23. How must a private pilot candidate be able to recognize that the airplane is in an unusual flight attitude?

    a) By comparing the position of the nose against the natural horizon.
    b) Solely by reference to the flight instruments.
    c) By sensing the feel of the flight controls and the sound of the engine.

24. The FAA-designated pilot examiner only cares that the airplane is returned to level flight. The sequence of the control application is not important.

    a) True.
    b) False.

Answers to Study Questions

1. c
2. a
3. a
4. get it back to straight-and-level flight as quickly as possible
5. a
6. c
7. high
   increased (or added)
8. a
9. a
10. b

11. ☐ Airspeed decreasing steadily
    ☒ Decreasing altitude
    ☐ VSI steady or indicating slight climb
    ☒ Airspeed increasing or above the desired airspeed
    ☐ Turn coordinator airplane banked to one side or the other
    ☐ Attitude indicator tumbled (or "spilled")
12. c
13. b
14. a
15. c

16.

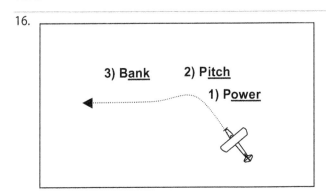
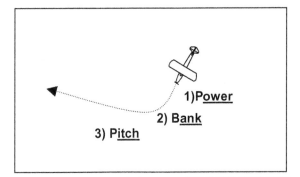

17. b
18. b
19. c
20. Fixation
21. a

22. b
23. b
24. b (false)

The Pilots Operating Handbook (POH)

READING ASSIGNMENT
Pilots Operating Handbook for your training airplane

Study Questions

(Note: POH contents vary considerably by airplane, so some of the following questions may not apply to your airplane. Ask your flight instructor for guidance.)

General POH Information

1. Each airplane, when built and certified as airworthy, is sold with an operating manual with the specific information for that specific airplane. What is that called?

   a) Owner's Guide to Operation (OGO).
   b) Pilots Operating Handbook (POH) or approved Airplane Flight Manual (AFM).
   c) User's Information Manual (UIM).

2. By law, this manual must be kept current and updated with any changes made to the airplane by the owner or manufacturer. Which of the following alterations to the aircraft do you think would merit changes made to the pages of the airplane flight manual? (Check all that apply.)

   ☐ Oil added to the engine oil reservoir
   ☐ Wheel fairings removed from the aircraft
   ☐ Engine replaced with larger engine
   ☐ Electric trim installed
   ☐ Both fuel tanks drained of fuel
   ☐ GPS unit installed

3. There can be multiple copies of the Pilots Operating Handbook (POH) made, however the original version has special legal significance. What do you think is true of the original?

   a) It is stamped with the aircraft tail number, and the aircraft is considered unairworthy if the original is not onboard.
   b) It is printed on buff colored paper to distinguish it from duplicates.
   c) It is permanently attached by secured cable to the aircraft.

4. If the original AFM is not onboard the aircraft, it is legal to fly provided the pilot has a commercially available aircraft information manual bought at an airport pilot shop.

   a) True.
   b) False.

5. What value are commercially available reprints of aircraft AFMs or POHs?

   a) They can be used to replace the approved original version in case of theft or loss.

   b) Pilots can use them to know exactly what equipment is installed on their specific training airplane.

   c) Pilots can learn much about the general equipment and performance capabilities of their training aircraft at home, without removing and possibly damaging the airplane's approved AFM.

6. A safe, competent pilot learns the capabilities of a new airplane by

   a) taking the airplane up on a test flight to learn by experience what the performance limits of the airplane are.

   b) obtaining a copy of the POH and studying it to understand the systems installed, their operating procedures and limitations, and the proper care and handling of the aircraft.

   c) working with a certificated aviation mechanic to dissemble the aircraft and view its structure and internal workings.

7. Unfortunately, there is little standardization of AFMs across aircraft manufacturers and, as a result,

   a) pilots must request from each manufacturer their official AFM structural design templates in order to know where important information is located.

   b) pilots have little or no way of finding important information in a timely manner.

   c) pilots should spend time reviewing a new AFM in order to determine where all critical information is located.

8. Next to each section description, identify which AFM section number in your POH it is referring to.

Description of the various engine, control, and environmental systems installed on the aircraft	_____
Step by step instructions for handing unusual or emergency situations that arise in flight	_____
Methods for servicing the aircraft, protecting it during ground handling, and keeping it if airworthy condition	_____
Specifications for operating limits that must not be exceeded	_____
Tables and charts showing the predicted performance of the aircraft in various flight environments	_____
Important information regarding the operation of systems installed after the aircraft was initially certificated	_____
The specific weight and center of gravity limits used to determine if the the aircraft has been loaded within operational limits.	_____

9. Identify in which POH section a pilot could find the following information.

_____ The speed at which to rotate the aircraft in a normal takeoff

_____ How the aircraft should be properly towed on the ground

_____ The speed at which to fly in an engine failure

_____ The maximum speed at which aircraft may be flown with the flaps extended

_____ The position of the center of weight of the fuel tanks used in determining the aircraft's loaded center of gravity

_____ The normal operating range for engine oil temperatures

_____ The expected fuel burn rate while cruising at 8,000 MSL

_____ A general, overall description of the powerplant

_____ A thorough description of the engine and related systems

_____ The proper operation of a newly installed GPS unit

10. For the purposes of preflight planning, when might a pilot use a commercially available POH?

   a) To check the specific operating capabilities of the aircraft.
   b) To determine the general operating capabilities of the aircraft.
   c) To calculate the exact weight and balance for the flight.

11. When should the pilot use the specific approved Airplane Flight Manual onboard the aircraft instead of a commercially available generic POH?

   a) For actual weight and balance information, and to confirm that the airplane's performance will be sufficient for the intended flight.
   b) For home study and general familiarization with the aircraft.
   c) For all flight training needs. Commercially available POHs have no information of value to a safe, competent pilot.

Your POH: General Section

12. Which is greater on your airplane, the length of the aircraft nose to tail, or the wingspan from wingtip to wingtip?

   a) The length.
   b) The wingspan.
   c) It varies depending on whether flaps are deployed.

13. If a ground obstacle such as a taxiway light stuck out of the ground by 18 inches, would your rotating propeller be able to clear the obstacle?

   _____

14. What is the manufacturer, model, and type of the engine installed on your training airplane?

_____

_____

_____

_____

15. The term "normally aspirated" refers to an engine that

    a) has aspirations of climbing to very high altitudes.
    b) rotates the propeller clockwise as seen from the pilot.
    c) uses air from outside the engine that has not been compressed ("turbocharged").

16. "Displacement" refers to

    a) the total volume displaced by the cylinders moving in and out, as they power the engine.
    b) the amount of air taken up by the engine block.
    c) the weight of the oil that is being moved throughout the engine.

17. Airplanes are designated as "high-performance" if the engine horsepower is greater than 200 horsepower. The most power output by the engine in your training airplane is _____, which is obtained when the engine is turning at _____ RPM.

18. Define the following terms:

    KIAS _____

    KCAS _____

    KTAS _____

    V_{NO} _____

    BHP _____

    Usable Fuel _____

    Standard Empty Weight _____

    _____

19. One hundred (100) nautical miles is equal to

    a) 85 statute miles.
    b) 105 statute miles.
    c) 115 statute miles.

20. How much is 15 °C in Fahrenheit?

    a) 48 °F.
    b) 59 °F.
    c) 98.6 °F.

Your POH: Limitations Section

 21. What do the airspeed limitations V_{NE}, V_{NO}, V_A, and V_{FE} have in common?

    a) They are the only V-speeds that begin with V.
    b) They vary with the total loaded weight onboard the aircraft.
    c) They define airspeed limits intended to prevent excessive stress being put on the airframe and powerplant.

22. Which represents a faster airspeed, V_{NO} or V_{NE}?

    a) V_{NO}.
    b) V_{NE}.
    c) It varies with the total loaded weight onboard the aircraft.

23. What V-speed matches up with the top speed of the white arc on the airspeed indicator?

    a) V_{NO}.
    b) V_A.
    c) V_{FE}.

24. What V-speed matches up with the top speed of the green arc?

    a) V_{NO}.
    b) V_A.
    c) V_{FE}.

 25. What is the static RPM range for your airplane, and what does that represent?

_____

_____

_____

26. What does the green arc represent on the oil temperature and oil pressure gauges?

    a) The normal operating range.
    b) The caution range.
    c) The oil temperature and pressure ranges with flaps extended.

27. Structurally, how could an airplane have a maximum ramp weight that is different from its maximum takeoff weight?

    a) Maximum ramp weight is determined by the speed at which the airplane taxies on the ground.
    b) Fuel weighs slightly less at altitude than it does on the ground.
    c) Ramp weight depends on the structural strength of the landing gear, and takeoff weight depends on the structural strength of the wings.

28. What is the maneuver speed limit for performing a steep turn in your airplane?

_____

29. Why is the total "usable" fuel capacity slightly less than the total fuel capacity?

a) A small portion of the fuel is used to fill the fuel lines, strainers, and reservoirs, and this portion should not be considered usable for flight planning purposes.
b) Combustion burns away a portion of the fuel.
c) The FAA requires aircraft manufacturers to round down all fuel capacities by 3%.

30. What color of aviation fuel are you allowed to use in your airplane?

a) Blue.
b) Blue and green.
c) Red and green.

31. In order to be airworthy, must the airplane have all of the placards listed in the POH displayed properly about the airplane?

_____

Your POH: Emergency Procedures Section

32. In an engine failure during flight, what airspeed should the pilot fly the airplane at?

a) V_{so}.
b) Maneuvering speed.
c) Maximum (or best) glide speed.

33. For what other situations might a pilot find procedures in Emergency Procedures Section of the POH? (Check all that apply.)

☐ Low oil pressure
☐ Engine fires
☐ Windshield damage, from a bird or other object
☐ Normal takeoff and landing
☐ Mixture leaning during cruise flight
☐ Electrical system malfunctions

34. Why are some steps in the Emergency Procedures Section bolded?

a) To indicate steps that are repeated multiple times as necessary.
b) To indicate steps that should be memorized by the pilot.
c) To indicate steps that are optional.

Your POH: Normal Procedures Section

35. For your airplane, which is a higher airspeed, V_X or V_Y?

_____

36. Why does the Normal Proceures Section include a procedure for doing a preflight inspection?

a) To communicate the items the manufacturer believes should be inspected prior to flight.
b) Because every pilot is required by law to follow the exact same steps while inspecting the airplane.
c) So that the mechanic performing the annual inspection will know what items to inspect.

37. By what method is the engine of your training airplane primed (some initial fuel added to the cylinders before starting)?

   a) With one or more pumps of the primer control.
   b) By engaging the auxiliary fuel pump, with coordinated use of the mixture control.
   c) The engine is never primed, even in cold weather.

Your POH: Performance Section

38. According to the POH, lowering the flaps changes the stall speed of the airplane.

   a) True.
   b) False.

39. Where did the manufacturer get the data used to create the charts and tables in the Performance Section?

   a) Copied from the POHs of other aircraft, because performance numbers are standardized.
   b) From many test flights of the aircraft under a variety of test conditions.
   c) Computer modeling.

Your POH: Systems Descriptions Section

40. How do motions of the control yoke translate into movements of the ailerons, elevator and rudder?

   a) Rigid control rods.
   b) Hydraulic lines.
   c) Cables.

41. While the aircraft is on the ground, how would the pilot steer to the left?

   a) By applying pressure on the left rudder pedal.
   b) By applying opposite rudder.
   c) By gently turning the control yoke to the left.

42. What does your POH recommend about the oil level in the engine for flights of extended length?

   a) The oil level should be above a higher minimum level for extended flights.
   b) For extended flights, pilots are advised to guard against excess oil at the start.
   c) The POH does not specify oil level differences by length of flight.

43. The aircraft electrical system consists of a _____ volt, _____ amp alternator or generator, and a _____ volt battery.

44. Does your aircraft have an ammeter or a loadmeter installed?

   a) An ammeter.
   b) A loadmeter.
   c) Both.

Your POH: Care and Handling Section

45. What FAA-required inspections are specified in the POH?

    a) Biennial inspection.
    b) Annual inspection (and 100 hour inspection if operated for hire).
    c) 2,100 hour engine and propeller inspection.

46. What covers, ties, and locks are listed in the POH tie-down procedures?

    a) Control wheel lock, tie-down ropes, and a pitot tube cover.
    b) Reflective windshield screen installed to protect aircraft avionics.
    c) Air intake blocks and a canopy rain cover.

47. In what POH section can pilots find the proper tire pressures to which the main wheels should be inflated?

    _____

Answers to Study Questions

1. b
2. ☐ Oil added to the engine oil reservoir
   ☒ Wheel fairings removed from the aircraft
   ☒ Engine replaced with larger engine
   ☒ Electric trim installed
   ☐ Both fuel tanks drained of fuel
   ☒ GPS unit installed
3. a
4. b (false)
5. c
6. b
7. c
8. varies by airplane, but for Cessna 172S:
   7
   3
   8
   2
   5
   9
   6
9. varies by airplane, but for Cessna 172S:
   4
   8
   3
   2
   6
   2
   5
   1
   7
   9
10. b
11. a
12. varies by airplane, but for Cessna 172S: b
13. varies by airplane, but probably not
14. varies by airplane, but for Cessna 172S: Lycoming IO-360-L2A engine, normally aspirated, direct drive, air-cooled, horizontally opposed, fuel injected, four cylinder engine with 360 cu. in. displacement.
15. c
16. a
17. varies by airplane, but for Cessna 172S: 180 bhp at 2700 RPM

18. knots indicated airspeed
    knots calibrated airspeed
    knots true airspeed
    structural cruising speed
    brake horsepower (power created by engine)
    fuel available for flight planning
    weight of standard airplane, with unusable fuel, full operating fluids, full engine oil
19. c
20. b
21. c
22. b
23. c
24. a
25. varies by airplane, but for Cessna 172S: 2300-2400 RPM, full throttle while stationary on the ground
26. a
27. c
28. varies by airplane, but for Cessna 172S: 95 knots
29. a
30. varies by airplane, but for Cessna 172S: b
31. yes
32. c
33. ☒ Low oil pressure
    ☒ Engine fires
    ☒ Windshield damage, from a bird or other object
    ☐ Normal takeoff and landing
    ☐ Mixture leaning during cruise flight
    ☒ Electrical system malfunctions
34. b
35. V_Y
36. a
37. varies by airplane, but for Cessna 172S: b
38. a (true)
39. b
40. varies by airplane, but for Cessna 172S: c
41. a
42. a

Answers to Study Questions

43. varies by airplane, but for 172S: 28 volt, 60 amp alternator, 24 volt batter

44. varies by airplane, but for 172S: a

45. b

46. varies by airplane, but for Cessna 172S: a

47. Section 8

About the Author

Dan Dyer is a certified flight instructor living and flying in the San Francisco Bay Area, rated in both airplanes and helicopters. He has been designated a Master CFI by the National Association of Flight Instructors (NAFI). He owns and operates San Carlos Flight Center, a flight school and aerial tours business located at San Carlos Airport.

Always learning himself, Dan loves to see flight instructors sharing their training methods with other flight instructors. Dyer Flight Training Tools is based on that vision, and the belief that effective learning can be fun. Dan can be reached at dan@sancarlosflight.com.

Dyer's VORs-At-A-Glance flash cards

Designed to show any pilot how to look at a VOR receiver and read it at a glance, these flash cards will teach you:

- The difference between VOR courses and VOR radials
- What the VOR does not show you
- Inbound vs. outbound course indications
- How to instantly know your position relative to the VOR
- Tricks for reading interception courses right off the VOR

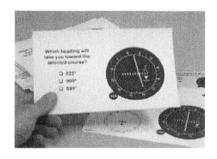

Ground School Workbook for Private Pilots
Flight Training Workbook for Private Pilots

These workbooks contain study questions and exercises tied to the FAA's primary training handbooks for private pilots – the Pilot's Handbook of Aeronautical Knowledge and the Airplane Flying Handbook.

- Draw your attention to the most important parts of the FAA materials
- Pull apart complex topics into easy-to-understand pieces
- Allow you to practice skills that require repetition
- Connect topics from across the FAA training materials
- The perfect companion to your flight instruction

Check us out at www.DyerFlight.com

CPSIA information can be obtained
at www.ICGtesting.com
Printed in the USA
BVOW09s0847191017

498030BV00003B/15/P